BLUE WATER SUMMER

A PACIFIC COASTAL KAYAK ADVENTURE

by David Johnston
& Krista Nicholson

ORCA PUBLICATIONS

Published in 1986 by
Orca Publications, Exeter, Devon.
Designed, Typeset and printed by
A. Wheaton & Co. Ltd.,
Exeter, Devon,
Great Britain.

ISBN 0 9511842 0 2

Dedicated to: Den and Jean and Russell and Jean.

ACKNOWLEDGEMENTS

To our sponsors, advisers and helpers.

Geoff McGladdery of Wye Kayaks, Andrew Ainsworth Designs Ltd., Optimus Ltd, John Dowd of Ecomarine, Vancouver, John Ramwell of A.S.K.C., Peter Salisbury of LRCC, Duncan Richards, Sue and Allen Slade in Vancouver, Edmund G. White, technical advisor, Outward Bound Mountain School, Ullswater, Janet Gibson of S.D.M.C., Ruth Treble and Karen Johnston **AND to all those who helped us on our way** Duncan and Fran in L.A., Ed the head in San Francisco, Steve and Mary Gropp on Orca's Island, Mrs Walkey in Vancouver, Ken, John and Kim in Bella Bella, Alex Murdoch and Family in Prince Rupert, Cec White in Sandspit, Kevin and Rob the 'Mad Brothers' of Vancouver, The 'Arctic Ocean' crew, The Five Fingers Lighthouse crew, The 'Observer' crew, Wally of Baranof, Bob, Dodie and Jay of cedar cove, Dale White, Eric and Joanne of Seattle, Jason of Seattle, Charlie and Cam of the 'Frontier Queen' in Juneau, Mark Skok of Anchorage, U.S. and Canadian Coastguards, B.C. Ferries and Alaska State Ferries.

CONTENTS

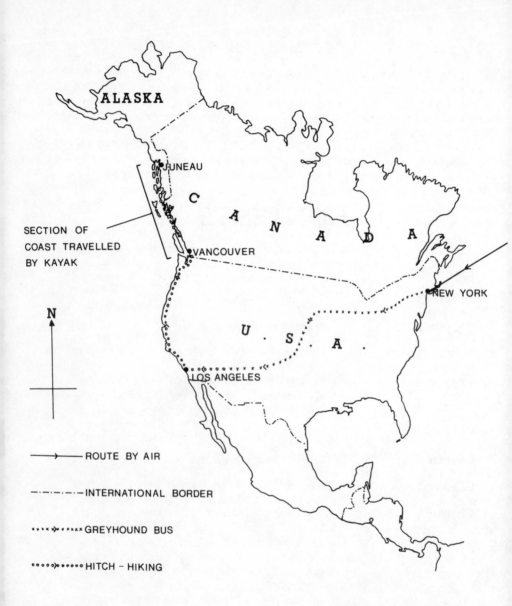

ALASKA

JUNEAU

SECTION OF
COAST TRAVELLED
BY KAYAK

C A N A D A

VANCOUVER

NEW YORK

N

U . S . A .

LOS ANGELES

———→——— ROUTE BY AIR

—·—·—·—INTERNATIONAL BORDER

××××✕×××××GREYHOUND BUS

°°°°°✕°°°°°HITCH – HIKING

Our route across North America to Vancouver

INTRODUCTION

The idea of a long kayak journey was conceived over a few pints in a Lake District pub, famous locally for its disregard of licensing hours.

At the time I was working as an instructor at Ullswater Outward Bound School, where I had met and become very friendly with Krista. As well as being good company she had a great sense of adventure and unfortunately for us her contract was rapidly coming to an end.

Over the riotous noise of the Public Bar we discussed our future and by the time we had left the pub our destiny had been decided. We were to accompany each other on a sea canoeing trip along the west coast of Canada to Alaska.

The news of our proposed trip soon reached the ears of our families, friends and acquaintances and their responses varied from enthusiastic encouragement to pessimistic discouragement.

Krista had a friend who manufactured and exported kayaks, so through him we arranged to have two kayaks sent to Canada. The plan was to take delivery of the boats in Vancouver, Western Canada, and then kayak north for 1,600 miles to Glacier Bay in Alaska.

We knew very little about the west coast but we had seen it in an Atlas and knew someone who had kayaked there and who strongly recommended it.

Our brief sponsorship campaign resulted in two free Primus stoves, free paddles and a pile of letters from firms regretting that they were unable to help us.

Neither of us had any experience of sea canoeing so we purchased a copy of John Ramwell's book on the subject and felt confident enough to be able to iron out any problems as they arose.

Early in the year our canoes were due to leave Liverpool for their six week jaunt across the globe to Vancouver and at about the same time we flew from England on a standby flight to New York.

We had originally intended to hitch hike across the States to California but that January New York was bitterly cold so we opted for the relative comfort of a Greyhound bus to take us across the Mid-West.

Sixty hours on the bus did us no good at all, jet lag coupled with a numb bum took its toll and Krista reacted with a severe attack of diarrhoea which lasted for 2,000 miles.

The only noteworthy excitement happened in New York when we were accosted by a tramp. He tried to intimidate us into giving him some money by rolling, what looked like, a live bullet around in his mouth. He then pointed it at us and threatened to bite it if we didn't give him some money. Judging that he would probably come off worst we left him to it.

Our hitch hiking started at Flagstaff in Arizona and our route took us to the Grand Canyon and then to Los Angeles. Once there we holed up for a week with some friends, and enjoyed the warm winter weather on the beach of Santa Monica. Our walks took us up the beach to Malibu and down beach to the boat owners' paradise of Delray Marina. After the snows of New York and the exhausting bus ride across the Mid-West, a walk along the palm fringed beaches in shorts felt like the ultimate pleasure.

It seemed rather odd to us, as we strolled past a prestigious Health Club, that people paid vast sums of money to walk on a conveyor belt in a sweaty gym, when outside they could have walked amongst the palm trees right next to the fabulous Pacific surf. Someone explained, 'They pay for being told to shed lard'.

On the day we left L.A. we encountered a film set and recognised the distinctive hair-do of 'Mr T.' of 'The A-team' fame. He was sat behind the wheel of a parked car, wiping his brow in readiness for another shoot. A monstrous camera was mounted on the car bonnet but as we ambled passed we didn't see any action.

The Santa Monica Freeway was not an easy place to hitch from so we walked along the shore, past the bronzed bodies on Muscle Beach, until the city traffic thinned out a little. A quick climb over the barrier, followed by an exciting crossing of eight lanes of traffic, landed us at a prime hitching spot.

Traffic from L.A. streamed past us at a fast and furious pace with nobody giving us a second glance, but after an hour or so our luck changed and a chauffeured limosine drew along side. The neatly dressed passenger pressed the button of his automatic window and enquired in a cultured accent as to whether we had any drugs. I told him that we hadn't and with a quick disinterested wave they went on their way.

Once out of Los Angeles travelling was less traumatic and in the following weeks we were able to see the sights of San Fransisco, and make a detour inland to the rock climbers' Mecca of Yosemite. Very few people were there that early in the year, and despite the season we enjoyed a full week of sunshine and clear blue skies.

Numerous trails fan out from 'The Valley' and wind up between the maze of vast granite walls. It was easy to see why this area appeals so much to climbers. Sheer rock faces of up to 3,000 feet in height rise impressively in all directions offering some of the most spectacular scenery in America. Because of its topography Yosemite is adorned with numerous waterfalls, including the third highest in the world. In one small area within the National Park there are six waterfalls over 1,000 feet high and two of these exceed 2,000 feet in vertical height.

Five weeks had passed since our arrival in New York, so we calculated that the kayaks would be arriving in Vancouver in a week's time. By allowing ourselves two weeks to get there we would create a week's leeway to absorb any unforseen delays in transportation.

From Yosemite we made a bee line for the Pacific Ocean and followed the Coast road north.

Good progress was made with liberal help from a bizarre collection of characters, including a trawler skipper who had to stop every few miles to heave up his breakfast, because he suffered from land sickness, and two country boys who were heading towards town to sell a sack full of home grown 'whacky tobaccy'!

On crossing the border into Oregon, the heavens opened and headway for the next 300 miles slowed to snail's pace. No one wanted two wet bodies in their car, so we stood in the rain, gradually turning from being mildly damp, to totally saturated! Camping was a problem, because we didn't have a tent, but somehow each evening we managed to find some kind of shelter, usually a bridge or a convenient tree.

By the fourth day of torrential rain, and after being drenched for the third time by a deliberate, car-induced, tidal wave, morale hit rock bottom. We were on the verge of crawling into the bushes, to die of hypothermia, when a car stopped and offered us a 360 mile lift, all the way to the Washington State Border.

By the time we got there, the wrinkles in our fingers had ironed out, and apart from the steam billowing from our clothes, we now looked and felt more human. Soon after stopping, another long lift hurtled us through Washington to Seattle.

Vancouver was now not much more than 100 miles away, and for the first time on our trip we felt that we were close to starting. To celebrate the end of a successful day, we booked into a small downtown hotel, and enjoyed the feeling of a dry bed and hot shower.

Rather than go directly by road to Vancouver, we chose a Ferry route that hopped through the San Juan Islands to Victoria on Vancouver Island. The reason for this was to visit some friends, and to get a mouth watering taster of the island-spattered coastline we would soon be canoeing through.

Steve and Mary Gropp live on Orca's Island at the head of Massacre Bay, in a wooden cabin that overlooks Skull Island. They proved to be a vast source of information in preparing for our coming adventure, as they had both travelled certain parts of the Canadian and Alaskan coastline in a wooden rowing boat. They told us about the tides, the danger areas, the bears, weather, water and even suggested a good route through the islands.

One evening they gave us a crash course on fire lighting in wet

Yosemite Falls, California

Christening the Kayaks in Vancouver

weather. Apparently mature spruce trees secrete a combustible sap from their bark, that can be used as a fire-lighter. We bombarded Steve and Mary with every unanswered question we could think of and, when we finally left Orca's Island, we had a revived sense of enthusiasm and could hardly wait to get going.

On 17th February we crossed into Canada, and after a day in the 'old town' of Victoria, we caught a ferry across the Straits of Georgia, to Vancouver.

Instead of rushing straight into town to collect the kayaks, we forced ourselves to rest for a few days, to recuperate from seven weeks of travelling through the States.

Later in the week we felt thoroughly rested so we caught a bus into town and rolled up at the Port of Vancouver Customs to collect the kayaks. They searched the entire holding warehouse, but no kayaks could be found. I knew that they were being transported on a ship called 'The American Express', so armed with that information, one of the senior officers sent off an enquiry telex.

A short while later came the devastating reply - the boats hadn't left Liverpool. We were speechless with shock! Industrial action at the docks had delayed loading, and 'The American Express' would not be leaving England for another week.

Our money supply was far too low to support us for seven weeks in Vancouver, so we set about looking for work. The whole situation was so frustrating, that after a while our sense of humour deserted us completely.

Krista had been born in Canada, so was able to apply for a work permit immediately and she soon landed a job waitressing in a delicatessen restaurant. I, on the other hand, had to search for slightly more illegal work.

In the evenings we sold circus tickets over the phone, and before long were breaking office records for circus ticket selling, by using a technique that involved varying degrees of moral blackmail!

We also ran an advertisement in a local paper offering a good quality, inexpensive interior decorating service. The first client didn't quite get the quality we had advertised, but he liked the price, and we were in business! Gradually the time went by with Krista waitressing during the week, helping me decorate at weekends and circus ticket selling in the evenings!

One of the few highlights of this phase of the expedition came when I accidentally over-charged someone for wallpaper stripping, and ended up earning $260 for half an hour's work!

Over all, our time in Vancouver was highly depressing, all our excitement had been quashed, and the wait for the kayaks seemed unending. Every week new delays occurred as 'The American Express' made its erratic course across the sea. Unscheduled stops, lay-overs and re-routes all added extra days on to our wait.

Our favourite walk in Vancouver was around the central recreation area of Stanley Park and it was from here that our wait came to a dramatic end. We were gazing out to sea one evening and there, amongst the ships moored at the entrance to the harbour, was 'The American Express'. 'It's here!' I shouted and we laughed, embraced, and patted each other on the back! It was as if a huge weight had been lifted from our shoulders and our sense of humour and enthusiasm returned once more.

I put the finishing touches to the Gynaecologist's surgery I was painting, and Krista handed in her notice at the delicatessen. Her boss asked why she was leaving, so Krista explained the canoe trip, and all he could say was 'I thought there was something odd about you!'

Over the following days the kayaks were unloaded and then held by customs for processing. Our boats had been shipped out amongst a larger batch of kayaks destined for a retail outlet. We managed to meet the importer who kindly offered us the use of his warehouse for our last few days of preparation. We were grateful for this, otherwise we would have been packing in the rain on a God-forsaken jetty.

We had a few days in hand now, with which to prepare for departure. Food supplies were the first major consideration, so we sat down and estimated how much food we would require for the entire journey. All the food had to be non-perishable, filling, nourishing, balanced and packaged in a way that would protect it from sea water, and enable it to fit into the limited space of the kayaks. Equipped with a shopping list, the proceeds of our telephone canvassing, and a large Yanky Mobile, we descended upon a bulk food store. The store displayed large vats of assorted food stuffs, and we were able to help ourselves to the necessary quantities of each item. Everything we bought was packaged in 1 kilogram lots, and double-bagged for strength. We filled trolley after trolley with food, as we worked our way around the store. Five kilos of brown rice, five kilos of white rice, five kilos of spaghetti, five kilos of macaroni, five kilos of assorted beans, another five of lentils, dried milk, sultanas, raisins, dried potatoes, and so the list went on. Through the assorted soup powders, dried vegetables, plain flour, wheat germ, wholemeal flour, porridge oats, rye flakes, oat flakes, bran, barley, drink crystals, thirty kilos of sugar, tea, drinking chocolate, pancake mix, peanuts, walnuts, pop-corn, sunflower seeds - and that was just the bulky food!

Smaller quantities of other basic foods were also bought, like salt, vinegar, cooking oil, lemon juice, spices, cornstarch, honey, jam, marmite and peanut butter.

Because of the nature of the trip and our mode of transport, tinned foods were impractical, but we did buy a few cans of peaches, pineapple, corned beef and sweet corn for treats.

Most of our fresh foods would have to be bought whenever possible on the way. Fresh fish we planned to catch, and we knew that most seaweed was edible if the worst came to the worst.

The food was unloaded back at the warehouse, and sorted out into piles. It would have been a physical impossibility to fit all the food into the boats at once, so we divided it into five equal parts. Each part represented one month's food. The first load was to be stowed in the boats for departure, and the other four were sent to different settlements on each stage of our route. The distance between each pick-up varied, so slightly larger or smaller parcels were sent, depending on the proximity of the next pick-up point. Canadian post is very reasonably priced, and we sent 4 x 120lb packages for less than the price of one at British postal rates!

Food organising, from buying to posting, took nearly two days, but we were more than glad of the chance to do something positive in the last few days of our marathon wait.

When the boats arrived at the warehouse, it was the first time we had ever seen them and it didn't take long to remove the protective wrapping of cardboard and polythene, revealing the sleek, classic lines of our new craft. At first sight they looked astonishingly beautiful. One was yellow and white and the other red and white, and they both gleamed under the warehouse lights. They had been skilfully constructed in fibreglass to our specifications by our friends at Wye Kayaks. They were 'Expedition Islanders', eighteen feet long and equipped with water-tight bulkheads to provide dry storage space and buoyancy. The decks sported small Union Jacks, deck lines and chart elastics for holding maps, compasses and other navigational instruments.

Access hatches to the water-tight compartments lay in the centre of the fore and aft decks, and were sealed neatly with tight fitting rubber caps. The cockpit was equipped with an adjustable foot rest, a comfortable seat and a pump. The bilge pump operated manually from the aft deck, and was designed to provide us with a quick and efficient method of pumping out the kayak in the event of a capsize. More elastics stretched across the rear deck to hold spare paddles and other equipment.

Most of our gear was sent with the kayaks, and it felt almost like Christmas, as we unloaded everything, to rediscover what we had packed for ourselves in England nearly four months previously.

There were clothes, tents, maps, paddles, stoves, buoyancy aids,

11

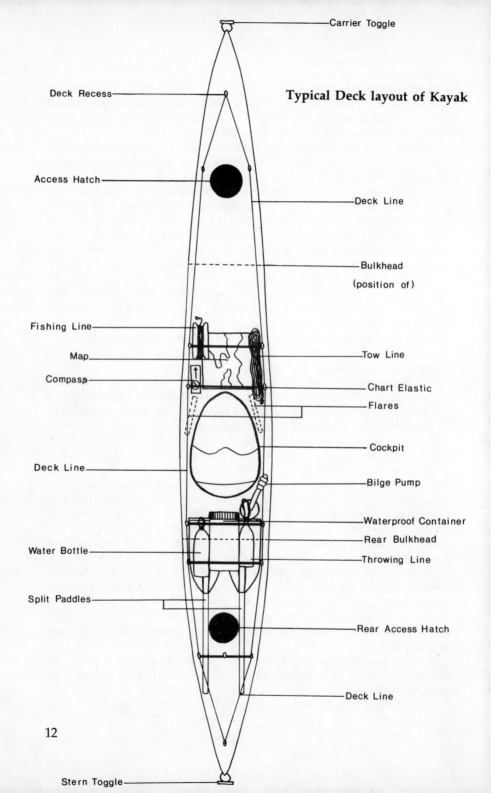

Carrier Toggle

Deck Recess

Typical Deck layout of Kayak

Access Hatch

Deck Line

Bulkhead
(position of)

Fishing Line

Map

Compass

Tow Line

Chart Elastic

Flares

Cockpit

Deck Line

Bilge Pump

Waterproof Container

Rear Bulkhead

Water Bottle

Throwing Line

Split Paddles

Rear Access Hatch

12

Deck Line

Stern Toggle

books, plates and cutlery, flares, repair kits, waterproofs, and most other things that we would conceivably need on the trip. The confused pile of food and equipment presented a daunting sight, and having never packed a sea kayak before, we were more than dubious as to whether it would all fit in. The answer was to ruthlessly discard any excess or useless items, and gradually whittle down the equipment to the bare necessities.

The only other equipment we had to buy included an extra fly sheet for the tent, an axe for splitting wet wood, an assortment of fishing tackle and a pair of sailing wellies to keep our feet dry.

Packing the boats for the first time took all day to perfect. Things that were needed regularly had to be close to the hatches, while other items had to be stowed well away. Equipment that did not need to be kept dry went in the cockpit, and the rest had to go inside the hatches. Some equipment was lashed to the decks for easy access, and all equipment in the cockpit had to be tied in, to avoid losing it in a capsize. The position of everything had to be memorised, and sensible consideration had to be given to the balance of each boat.

Throughout the day the kayaks were loaded, re-arranged and adapted until every piece of food and equipment had a place to go. It was like a giant 3-dimensional jigsaw puzzle, with pieces of irregular shape and size that had to be interlocked in the best possible way.

When we had finished packing, each kayak weighed 300lb. That evening we gave them a float test, and despite the weight, they actually did! We then took them out for a spin around Vancouver Harbour and the first thing that struck me was their stability. They were so bottom-heavy that capsizing would need some real effort. The upturned sweeping bow sliced through the choppy water with immense ease and a good cruising speed was easy to maintain. They were also directionally stable which meant that we wouldn't lose momentum and rhythm by constantly having to use compensating strokes. Nearer to shore we tested their manoeverability between the moored boats, and were well pleased with the versatility and agility of our new kayaks. They would be equally as good either close to shore or on long crossings.

Towards the end of our test run we decided to pop in and see John Dowd at the Ecomarine Canoeing Shop at the harbour's edge. As we pulled up to the jetty, we noticed another canoeing couple walking slowly away from their moored kayaks. We landed and the girl turned around. She blinked, let out a shriek and screamed 'Krista!' Krista shrieked 'Marguerite!' and they both ran towards each other and shrieked together! Marguerite is one of Krista's best friends whom she hadn't seen for well over a year, and here, totally out of the blue, on one of hundreds of jetties in Vancouver, they met!! She had heard

13

about our trip through the grapevine, but thought she was about a month too late to meet us. Her companion, Stuart, had by coincidence also worked in Outward Bound Centres but mainly in Canada.

They had hired some boats for the day from Ecomarine, so we invited them out with us on the first day of our trip. They accepted, and re-hired the kayaks for another two days.

It was getting dark, so we arranged a meeting time for an evening drink and paddled back to our launch pad. The owner of the landing pontoon allowed us to leave our kayaks on the jetty overnight so we tied them together, secured a tarpaulin over the cockpits, and left, happy in the knowledge that tomorrow our journey was due to begin.

From then onwards, we both intended to keep a daily diary and thus keep a record of our first adventure together...and so our expedition begins...

Chapter One: **Teething Troubles**

Day 1 14th April

Sheer excitement got us out of bed early, and straight after breakfast we carried the kayaks to the launch pad, and waited in the sun for Marguerite and Stuart to arrive.

They were delayed for a while, because their car had been towed away, but eventually they arrived at the jetty with a boat full of beer. Sue Slade took some photographs to mark the end of our frustrating wait, and the boats were christened in regal style with a spray of beer. Our biceps were measured for scientific purposes and, soon after, our cheery quartet paddled out of Vancouver Harbour. We passed Stanley Park, and the point at which we first spotted 'The American Express', and continued along the built-up shoreline of North Vancouver.

A lighthouse at Point Atkinson marked, for us, the outer limits of Vancouver, so it seemed appropriate to stop and celebrate our departure, by landing on the rocks below the lighthouse to crack open a can of beer!

We decided to stop for the evening on a large island in Howe Sound, called Bowen Island because it overlooked the city. The four mile crossing from the lighthouse started well, but right in the middle a wind whipped up, and the tide began to run. Krista and I lost contact with Marguerite and Stuart, and slowly began to realise that we were being swept out of Howe Sound into the Straits of Georgia.

We battled to regain control of our direction, and as we got closer to Bowen Island, Krista became caught in a strong tide race. We were both concerned about her lack of forward movement, and were forced to back away into deeper water to overcome the obstacle.

We met up with Marguerite and Stuart again at the island, and chose to land and camp for the night on a small beach. While Krista and I were hauling our boats, over the tangle of logs on the beach, to above the high tide mark, we began to realise how difficult it was to manoeuvre boats weighing 300lbs over slippery rocks. Camping, we knew, would be difficult, but this was ridiculous! It took 2½ hours to set up camp, and secure the boats above the high tide mark.

Food and equipment was so carefully packed that we couldn't remember where certain vital items were. A full scale search had to be mounted right through the boats to find them and once we had unpacked, our biggest fear was not being able to get everything back in. Meanwhile, Marguerite and Stuart watched, bemused by our blatant inexperience.

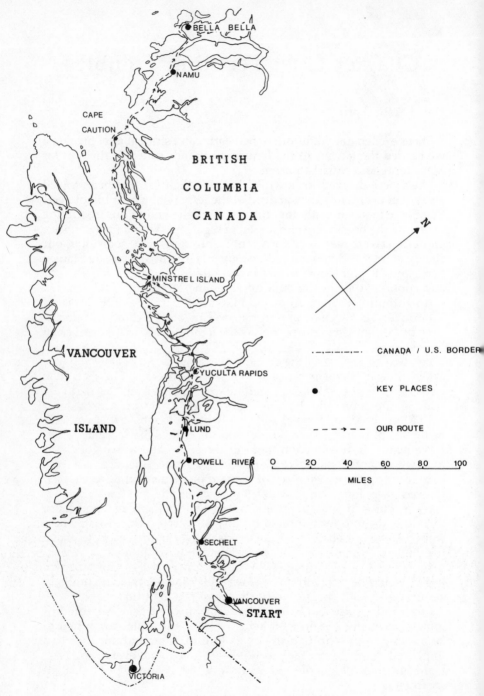

BELLA BELLA

NAMU

CAPE
CAUTION

BRITISH

COLUMBIA

CANADA

MINSTREL ISLAND

N

VANCOUVER

YUCULTA RAPIDS

—·—·—·—·— CANADA / U.S. BORDER

● KEY PLACES

ISLAND

LUND

— — —→— — OUR ROUTE

POWELL RIVER

0   20   40   60   80   100

MILES

SECHELT

VANCOUVER
START

VICTORIA

16

The route from Vancouver to Bella Bella

Everyone was tired after the days efforts and in the evening we relaxed around a hearty campfire, watching the lights of Vancouver shimmer in the distance.

Day 2 15th April

A miserable drizzle greeted us in the morning and, as expected, the breaking of camp and boat packing was slow and frustrating.

Stuart and Marguerite waited patiently at the water's edge for us while we manhandled our overweight kayaks, across the slippery log choke, to the sea. Boat-carrying was obviously going to be a major chore.

Once on the water however, the tide was with us, and our mood changed from near disillusionment to one of sheer delight. We paddled as a four until midday, alongside the rock fringed spruce forests of Bowen Island and parted company with our two friends over a large lump of cooking chocolate. A feeling of solitude overtook us as they waved their last farewells, and for the first time we were able to savour the feeling of an imminent adventure together.

Several bald eagles watched us cruise by from their perches high in the trees, and at one point we drew close to what looked like a gnarled floating log of driftwood, which suddenly splashed to life. We had disturbed a dozing sea lion, who snorting noisily swam towards Krista with its head high out of the water. We backed off nervously, unsure of its intentions, and thankfully the sea lion did the same. After a few seconds he dived, and we didn't see him again.

To avoid lugging the heavily laden boats to the campsite we tried taking most of the bulky food and equipment out first, and carrying it up the beach in small batches before returning for the kayaks. In theory the idea sounded pretty good, but in practice, the tide came in so fast that we ended up running up and down the beach in blind panic, trying to keep everything away from the rising water!

Information we had received before setting out from Vancouver included advice about protecting food from rodents, bears and other creatures which are reputed to be capable of devouring the entire contents of human food caches. To avoid this we were told that all food should be hung at least 15ft in the air and well away from any tree trunk.

Like good Boy Scouts we filled a tarpaulin with all our food, and carried the load to the base of our chosen tree. A strong looking bough protruded from the trunk several yards above the ground and, because the trunk was too wide to climb, we took it in turns throwing a weighted line over the branch. Eventually one good shot succeeded in looping the branch, and soon we had the tarpaulin tied to the end. We both grabbed the line and heaved with all our might, but the rope was too thin, and it cut into our hands, without the food showing even a hint of ascending. Unanimously, we voted to kick the project in the teeth, and stow everything back in the boat for the night.

One of the pleasant things about the beaches in this part of the world was the amount of seasoned driftwood that found its way on to them and, after the rigours of the food-hanging fiasco, we were glad of the chance to relax and reflect on the day by the warmth of a roaring fire.

Day 3 16th April

Every movement we made around our morning campsite was carefully monitored by an inquisitive seal, that floated buoy-like a safe distance off shore. Its shining, unblinking eyes glimmered above the grey water, never once glancing away. Perhaps, it was because of our attentive audience, that we packed so efficiently today!

Only when we launched the kayaks did it take fright and splash away. Eight miles of gentle paddling took us through the large islands of Howe Sound to a small settlement named Gibson's Landing. We found an empty docking pontoon between the fishing craft and float planes, and went in search of a general store.

We bought a pulley to assist with food hanging, in the unlikely event of us trying again, and the friendly storekeeper talked to us about whale migration. Apparently at this time of the year, killer whales congregate at a place called Robson Bight on Vancouver Island and to get there he suggested that we put the kayaks on a ferry and re-launch on arrival. We left Gibson Landing heartened by the friendliness of the locals, and relieved that the big city was comfortably behind us.

The good thing about starting our journey from Vancouver, and heading north between the mainland and Vancouver Island, was that we were in close proximity to the road, for the first 100 miles. It was in these early stages that teething troubles were most likely to occur, and the road provided us with a reassuring safety link in the event of an emergency. By the time we reached the road head we should be aware of our limitations and confident enough not to need an easy escape route.

Most of the wood on our camping beach was wet, so we tested the axe for the first time, and were pleased with the results. The bone dry core wood was easily exposed with a well placed blow, and it readily split into thin strips for kindling.

Evenings by the fire and close to the water's edge were always pleasant, but this evening was superb, for we had a pastel-coloured view of the snow-capped mountains of Vancouver Island.

Krista cooked an excellent meal of freshly-picked mussels, and it felt good to be together.

Day 4 17th April

To avoid having to carry the boats too far we made an early start and launched at high tide. My arms felt heavy all morning and, judging by our lack of forward movement Krista's were feeling the same.

In the afternoon a stiff breeze and a choppy swell developed and as the wind increased it became more and more difficult to keep on course. The wind was blowing at forty five degrees to the bow, and the kayaks, as with all small craft, had a tendency to veer into the wind, making forward paddling strenuous on one arm. Our arms weren't used to this sort of continuous exercise, and our paddling technique was too basic to cope safely with the conditions. So shouting through the wind and spray we decided to land on the nearest island before one of us capsized.

With relief, we landed on the lee side of Trail Island and stumbled ashore. It turned out to be a camper's dream, plenty of dry driftwood, soft places to pitch a tent, fabulous views all around, and the whole island was no more than 75 yards in length.

Day 5 18th April

The wind increased further during the night making the sea rough and confused. In normal circumstances we would have stayed on the island, but on this occasion we were forced to leave because we had no water. Trail Island was far too small to have a stream so our only choice was to paddle the mile to the mainland.

We launched in the relatively calm water on the sheltered side of the island but, within minutes, we were engulfed in chaotic waves. The stability of the boats inspired confidence, even in these irregular conditions, but we both found steering appallingly difficult. Our intended course took us broadside to the wind, and consequently

19

nearly every stroke became either a support or energetic steering stroke. The spray whipped up around us and progress was painfully slow. After an hour of hectic canoeing we managed to land, thoroughly exhausted on the mainland. It had been the most traumatic mile of the trip so far, but, once we had recovered from the ordeal, we dragged the boats up the sand, secured them and went in search of water.

The road wasn't too far away, so we took a walk for a couple of miles through a corridor of wild, whistling trees to the town of Sechelt. Most of the houses appeared to be summer homes for wealthy Vancouvans and there were few people about. A picturesque lagoon nestled behind Sechelt which played host to several stilted wooden jetties, float planes and fishing boats. Apparently, further north, tarmac runways are few and far between and most aircraft have to rely on floats for landing. The peacefulness of the harbour belied the ferocity of the wind on the coastal side of Sechelt and after some time amongst the fishing boats we walked back, against the wind, to the kayaks.

Once there we settled down to an early evening meal and by the time it was over the wind had miraculously dropped. The grey clouds that covered the sky earlier in the day also disappeared revealing a warm, evening sun. The sudden and unexpected wind abatement encouraged us back into the canoes and we returned to our previous campsite on Trail Island.

Because of the bear hazard along our proposed route we had been advised to camp, whenever possible, on small islands. This was because small islands with no streams could not sustain a bear, thus theoretically reducing the chance of an encounter. However, because an island was small, didn't necessarily mean that it was bear free. Bears are good swimmers and have been known to drag deer carcasses across several miles of water in order to keep it from falling prey to other bears.

Small islands during these first few days meant, for us, peace of mind and a good sleep.

Day 6   19th April

At this time of the year the weather seemed to follow a vague pattern. As usual we set off in calm conditions and an hour or so later the wind began to blow. As soon as the breeze arrived Krista's steering went badly up the shute and she became tired and frustrated. We could do nothing about it except hope that in time, our techniques would improve.

At lunchtime we stopped in a rocky bay known as Smugglers Cove, where we found oysters laying in deep clutches between rocks and on the beaches. While I lit the fire in a sheltered spot, Krista set about harvesting some for lunch. Wind-sculpted trees kept the chilly breeze from us and we huddled near the fire to eat our fill.

At the end of the day we both felt weak and tired from the constant grind of canoeing against the wind and we were glad to turn into a calm channel. We followed it for two miles before it occurred to us that we were paddling into a dead-end inlet and not through a channel. In our state of mind this seemed like the end of the world and, thoroughly depressed, we turned round and weakly paddled the two miles back again.

When looking ahead at the daunting thought of five months canoeing, negative progress was psychologically hard to cope with, especially after finding the first few days unexpectedly hard.

At the entrance to the inlet we stopped to set up camp and while securing the boats to a suitable tree we were halted in our tracks by a loud rustling sound which quickly became louder and louder. Something in the forest was coming straight at us and we had no idea what it could be. In a flurry of leaves it burst into view and we heaved a sigh of relief. It was a large, short-sighted beaver. It continued to walk towards us and ambled straight between us before it realised we were there. Startled by the sudden knowledge of our presence, it bolted, panic stricken, to the sea where it spent the entire evening swimming back and forth waiting for us to depart. Although being told that beavers don't enter the sea, there was no mistaking that it was a beaver by its distinctive flat, paddle-like tail.

Day 7 20th April

Every day so far we have seen seals, and they seem to find particular interest in our land based activities, often staring for long periods from their safe watery vantage points. Their large, shiny eyes followed us everywhere as if they were worried they might miss something.

Today we covered ten miles, again against a menacing headwind. Poor old Krista had steering problems, and we both found that our wrists were beginning to ache from the constant paddling of the heavily laden boats. The development of sore wrists was a bad sign and we were concerned as to whether they would hold out for the entire journey. If they were giving trouble after a few days, what would they be like in five months!

Concern over sore wrists may sound like chronic hypochondria but there is a complaint common to canoeists called teno-synovitis, that can devastate a long canoe trip. It is caused by excessive twisting and

21

pulling on the wrists and quite simply, the lubricating fluid inside the tendon sheath dries up, causing the tendon to rub painfully inside. In the event of developing teno-synovitis the only remedy is total rest for up to one month. To prevent the potential failure of the trip, we decided that we would stop for a day or two if our wrists ever became too sore. Other ways of avoiding extra strain, were to loosen one's grip on the paddle and to lessen the twisting action by using unfeathered blades.

Over supper we pondered on our canoeing styles and came up with a startling and embarassing revelation. For seven days we had been holding our paddles upside down!! Our paddle blades were assymetric and after trying a few practical experiments, we realised that using an upside-down assymetric blade caused an unnatural twisting, which in turn would create more tension in the wrist at each stroke.

Day 8 21st April

The wind was buffeting the tent in the morning so I crawled outside and climbed a nearby hill to inspect the sea conditions. It was exactly as I expected, so I returned to bed and had a lie in.

During the course of the morning the barometer gradually rose, and by early afternoon the wind had dropped to a friendly breeze. Revitalised by our rest, we launched again and continued northwards up Georgia Strait.

We were now in sight of Texada Island, the largest island in the strait, which is situated midway between Vancouver Island and mainland Canada. We were told that none of the local Indians ever go there, because legend says that the island rose suddenly out of the sea and they believe, that one day it may sink back just as quickly!

Krista was not as tired as she had been yesterday, and we canoed strongly north westwards with our paddles the right way up.

On the way we saw sea otters, swimming in close groups, and several bald eagles watched vigilantly from the tree tops. Over the past few days we had heard a strange sound coming from the sea on several occasions, and we couldn't discover what it was. It sounded like a hammer banging on a nail, in short rhythmic bursts and it was only when we saw a sea otter making the sound that we realised what it was. Sea otters feed on shellfish and to break the shell, they float on their backs with the shell balanced on their chest. They then hit it repeatedly with a stone until it cracks, hence the strange sound.

Sea otters are highly amusing and playful creatures and they seemed

22

completely unperturbed by our presence. They are larger than river otters and have a thick coat of coarse hair. They recline almost human-like, amongst the floating seaweed and watch nonchalantly as we paddle by.

Towards the end of the day we turned a corner and were startled by the alarmingly loud barking of four hefty sea lions. They were lying on an isolated rock and made it quite clear that they didn't want us too close. Having only seen circus sea lions before, their huge size took us by surprise and we gave them a wide berth.

We made camp on a beach six miles short of Powell River, the first and last town of any size on the road north of Vancouver.

Day 9 22nd April

A strong wind and rain blew up during the night and continued to lash down all day. Canoeing was out of the question because the sea was too rough and the wind far too strong. We opted for another late breakfast and contemplated our lack of progress.

Back in the tent, Krista surprised me by producing an Easter egg that she had stowed secretly since Vancouver. We made short work of devouring it before getting down to the serious business of lighting a fire.

On this particular day it presented us with a real challenge. The wood was wet, the wind howling, and the rain was pouring down. It took a solid hour, of gentle nursing, before the fire really got going but once a good flame had taken hold it really began to roar. Fuelled by excessive wind it quickly ate through the large logs, radiating heat towards us and showering the beach downwind with fast moving sparks.

We set up the tarpaulin near the fire, to keep the rain off, and to provide us with an alternative shelter, away from the confines of the tent. A tarpaulin made such days far more bearable and, if erected correctly, could be useful for catching rain water.

We were now within striking distance of both Powell River and Lund. Lund was significant because it marked the last tarmac link with civilisation for the next 500 miles to Prince Rupert.

From then onwards we would be largely on our own, relying on each other, and without the comfort of being within easy reach of a road.

Day 10 23rd April Easter Monday

An extra early start was made to capitalise on the morning calmness, but soon after leaving the beach, the horizon began taking on the tell-tale darker hue of an approaching wind. Within minutes it hit us, head on, with an icy blast. It was unexpectedly cold and we were forced to wear windproof over-mitts to keep the wind and spray at bay.

It was hard work paddling at snail's pace against the wind but eventually the six miles were covered and we slid into the sheltered waters of West View commercial fishing harbour.

We tied the boats to a vacant jetty and walked into Powell River where we thawed out over eggs on toast.

Powell River boasts the largest pulp and saw mill in the world, and its tall red and white chimneys were the most prominent feature in town.

The main topic of conversation was the impending redundancies at the mill, due to falling demand and financial cutbacks. As most people in Powell River have some sort of connection with the mill, their concern was understandable and a possible answer to the problem was explained on the toilet wall of the restaurant. It read, in bold black letters, 'SAVE THE MILL - WIPE TWICE' !!

Back at the harbour we were surprised to find a small crowd gathered around our boats. They all seemed interested in the trip but dubious that we would finish it. For the rest of the morning we chatted, over tea and biscuits, with a friendly couple who lived aboard a converted tug. They knew the coast well and gave us vital information about the tidal rapids we would encounter further up the coast.

Our paddle against the persistent wind continued in the afternoon, in an attempt to clear Powell River and find a suitable campsite.

On the outskirts of town, vast log booms floated behind a screen of scuttled ship hulks, to await processing at the mill. The hulks form a barrier to contain the logs but, on the outside, their high vertical sides reflected and magnified the swell, causing unnerving wave clapotis. Undercurrents drained beneath the hulks to the logs beyond, which posed a serious threat to a swimmer. For this reason the 'roller coaster' of a ride round the ships proved to be a highly unnerving event. Our headway around the logs was agonisingly slow and this didn't do much to boost our confidence, especially when my water container was washed off the deck and got sucked under a hulk to the logs beyond. It was comforting to know that the kayaks were good performers because we could not afford to capsize.

Just beyond Powell River we struck camp in a cove called Scuttle Bay.

Day 11 24th April

A clear dawn offered us superb views of Vancouver Island across the blue seas of Georgia Strait. The weather was again windy but clear and bright. Because of the wind we made little headway, so we beached some two miles further on in a cosy little suntrap and decided to dedicate the day to letter writing. A local lady spoke to us and invited us in to use her shower and have a cup of tea.

The stretch of coast between here and Vancouver, she explained, was affectionately known as the 'Sunshine Coast', because it lies in the rain shadow of the 5,000 foot peaks of Vancouver Island.

We were very lucky to stop at this particular spot, because not only did we meet the lady who offered us a shower but we also met a man from South Wales who worked at the mill. He gave us two beers each and let us sleep in his spare cabin for the night. This meant that we could pack the boats fully in the evening, to ensure a bright early start to beat the morning wind.

It was here, whilst busy writing letters, that we first noticed a most unexpected form of wildlife. The trees were alive with what seemed to be large bees. On closer inspection, the 'bees' turned out to be humming birds, which were hovering and flying haphazardly amongst the branches. Until now I had always thought that they were a tropical South American bird. They have a metallic sheen, are about 2½ inches long, with a straight bill and the wings move so rapidly that they appear invisible. They were fascinating birds to watch and were surprisingly tame. They hover, sometimes in dozens, and feed unconcerned by close human presence. They migrate northwards in the summer as far as the Alaskan pan handle.

Day 12 25th April

We rose early to beat the wind and we arrived at Lund, canoeing via an island named Dinner Rock. The rock was smooth and dome-shaped with a solitary cross perched on the top. The cross commemorated a shipwreck early this century, from which all were saved except for a baby who tragically drowned. To this day the family maintains the cross in memory of the baby.

The fact that Lund marked the road head was confirmed by a large sign which announced 'THIS IS THE END OF HIGHWAY 101'. For the next 500 miles northwards, all coastal settlements are serviced by sea and air only.

We sampled the coffee in the Fisherman's Bar until we had warmed up sufficiently to slide back into our kayaks and paddle slowly away from our tarmac umbilical cord. The beach front properties, that had adorned the coast up to Lund, were now conspicuous by their absence, and our isolation, at last, was beginning to feel complete.

We rounded Sarah Point, out of Georgia Strait, in a hectic tide race and entered Desolation Sound. It felt more remote than ever here, because we were now out of sight of the occasional tug or ferry on the main shipping routes of Georgia Strait.

Camp was struck on a small unnamed island which was surrounded by purple, clinging star fish. In the evening I tried fishing for the first time, but with no luck or, more to the point, no skill!!

For the next few days we shall be canoeing, clear of the main shipping routes, through a network of channels and islands that dissipate into the Pacific at Queen Charlotte Sound, north of Vancouver Island.

Day 13   26th April

For the first time on the trip there was no wind and the sun felt warm so, to celebrate our change of fortune, we opted for a slow start. The water was perfectly calm and we had mesmerising views of mountains, islands and channels, all with perfect reflections. The white angular peak of Mount Gilbert was particularly impressive, and dominated the skyline with its size and shape.

We were now in Desolation Sound, so named by Capt. Vancouver in the 1790's when he was searching for the North-west passage. It appeared to him as being the most desolate place on earth. Understandably so in his position, because he was navigating through uncharted waters and from the Sound, numerous channels radiate in various directions, all of which had to be explored to find the key passage. With incessant rain, wind and mist limiting his visibility to a few yards, it was not hard to imagine why the Sound was so named.

On our trip it was different, and proved to be the best place yet for oysters. Unfortunately, we had eaten so many over the last few days that, we couldn't face any more so we had a change to mussels.

We promised ourselves a rest at Desolation Sound for a day or two, so we paddled unhurriedly together, admiring the rich, scented pine forests and absorbing the magnificence of the scenery we were temporarily a part of. On our way we were met by a friendly couple in a speed boat. One of them had seen us on Monday from a fire engine, which was parked near the Powell River log booms. He told us that he had looked the other way when he saw us paddling, round the hulks, against the wind because he was sure we were in difficulties.

We asked them to teach us the best way to catch fish and they gave us some helpful hints before hurtling off southwards. I put their hints to the test and within minutes I caught the first cod of the trip. A strong line was used with a lure secured at the end. A three-pronged hook was connected to the lure and the whole thing lowered to the sea bottom. It was then pulled up to about three feet from the sea bed, and jigged with sharp, arm-length jerks. After each jerk it sinks at its own speed and is jigged again. We were told to continue jigging for about two minutes and if nothing bit they were either not feeding or there were no fish around. Rock cod are bottom fish and the best spots for catching them were next to steep cliff faces that descend directly into the sea. The ideal depth was between 35 and 100 feet and if nothing bites after a few minutes, they suggested that we paddle a few strokes further on and try again.

We camped on another unnamed island in the evening and experimented on the most effective way of gutting the fish. Rock cod are an ugly fish with sharp spines on the dorsal fin which have a poisonous coating on their tips, so care had to be taken to avoid a painful jab.

Day 14   27th April

Today was a rest day so we rose at a leisurely hour and had a long, slow breakfast. Our water supply was low, so after breakfast we canoed about three miles, across calm water, to the nearest stream which was situated at the end of a high sided inlet called Roscoe Bay. We filled our containers from a lake that nestled like a jewel in the wooded hills. It was only visible from the air or by those lucky enough to be able to walk there. The water appeared jet black, reflecting the mighty trees to perfection. A choke of well-preserved logs blocked the outflow, their size bearing testimony to the strength and magnificence once possessed by these fallen giants. The stillness in this natural haven was overwhelming and we sat in silence, feeling rather humble, realising that there were thousands of other such lakes in Canada, all just as capable of making such a profound impression.

On the return paddle we spotted two porpoises swimming side by side, rising gracefully to the surface with a light puff of exhalation. They arched on the surface several times before disappearing from sight.

Krista developed a sore arm but apart from that we had both benefitted from the day off.

Hair wash on the Sunshine Coast

A calm day in Desolation Sound

Day 15 28th April

Another day of leisurely canoeing, in the sun, took us the seven miles to Refuge Cove. Refuge Cove is a minute settlement consisting of a store, a floating fuel dock, a handful of houses and a resident sea plane. There was virtually no sign of life when we arrived, so I went fishing in the Bay while Krista went to explore the village. She returned half an hour later with a crab trap and a cod lure so that we could double our fishing potential. We chose a small island in Refuge Cove for our camp and, because the weather had been so dry and warm for the past three days, the fire was easy to start. I went off to erect the tent on a nearby rise when I heard Krista in a remarkably calm voice shout, 'Dave, will you come and help me to put this fire out?' I dashed over the rocks towards her and was aghast to see a blanket of flames sweeping rapidly in all directions, and burning the crisp, dry lichen that covered the rocks. Smoke billowed and flying sparks began igniting other areas and only after some vigorous tap dancing amongst the flames did we manage to bring it under control, at the dire cost of melting my wellies.

Day 16 29th April

We departed from our, now partially vegetated, island to search for water. From the map we chose a stream which was shown to be flowing out of Thompson Lake. We soon discovered that the stream did not exist, so we fought our way through the forest towards the lake. Hidden rustlings echoed deep in the trees which gave us the creeps and made our imaginations run riot. We were quite certain that we were surrounded by bears. The forest eventually cleared at the lake and it looked almost identical to the Black Lake that we had visited two days earlier.

Whilst stooping to fill our water containers we startled a vividly coloured, yellow and black water snake which, in its fright, wriggled quickly across the lake away from us. Once it was a good distance away we continued to fill our containers and made our way back to the boats.

Relieved to be out of the rustling forest, we launched and continued canoeing until lunchtime when we found a beach called Oyster Ledge. Shellfish grew in profusion here so while we fed ourselves with one hand, the other dug for clams and within a few minutes we had collected enough for a meal.

Most clams live in sand and consequently contain a lot of grit. Before eating them, it is necessary to soak them in clear sea water, to enable them to flush out the sand from their systems. Consuming grit leaves one susceptible to appendicitis so we usually allowed 24 hours for them to have a thorough rinse before eating them.

A sealed plastic bag filled with clear sea water was the most practical way of keeping clams and it could easily be secured to the deck. On flat stretches we tried keeping them in an open saucepan, on the deck, but we gave this up after being squirted every few minutes by over enthusiastic clams.

After a brief lunch stop we turned into the narrow waters of Lewis Channel and paddled immediately into a headwind. At the end of the channel we waited for the wind to abate before crossing three miles of open water to the Rendezvous Islands.

I caught a huge ling cod at the first island and, because we hadn't yet devised a means of landing or killing fish from the kayak, Krista had to tow me about a mile, to the nearest landing spot, while I controlled the fish. Using our present techniques it was impossible to paddle and control a fish at the same time. It was also unwise to put it in the cockpit because, apart from getting slapped on the inside of your legs, the fishy smells might attract bears.

We camped on the third Rendezvous Island in a secluded bay with a good supply of wood. I decapitated the fish with our trusty axe and Krista used the head as bait in the crab trap.

Day 17 30th April

It rained and rained throughout the night and in the morning we prised ourselves reluctantly from our sleeping bags and paddled in a grey drizzle towards the notorious Yuculta Rapids.

These rapids are a tide water torrent, caused by a large body of water being forced through a narrow channel every time the tide floods or ebbs. The Yucultas are by no means the fastest tidal rapids in the area, but they are the most notorious. They run at a speed of about nine knots as opposed to other rapids in the area that attain speeds of twelve to sixteen knots.

Ever since leaving Powell River people have been warning us about the Yucultas. A few years ago a tug overturned in the rapids drowning the whole crew. Several years before that a film crew, making a documentary about early pioneers, attempted to negotiate the rapids in a large Indian style canoe. It capsized and all seven occupants were drowned.

These warnings and stories made us realise that the Yucultas required

30

great respect. With a sense of impending doom, we approached the rapids cautiously, giving the mouth a wide berth to avoid being sucked down prematurely. Through the misty drizzle five or six pairs of Dall porpoises swam lazily around, looking like black, heavily-set dolphins. They appeared in all directions but never approached within thirty yards of us. Apparently they wait outside the rapids for an easy feed on dazed fish. Even whales have been known to wait outside the rapids for slack tide, before atttempting to pass through on their migratory routes.

We stopped first, at Stewart Island to inspect the rapids before venturing onto the water and near our landing spot six bald eagles were picking at a badly shredded fish head. As we approached they flew into some nearby pine trees and waited patiently for us to leave.

It was best to negotiate rapids at slack water, so we waited for an hour in the rain for the tide to slow down and amused ourselves by watching the seagulls drift elegantly by.

About ten minutes before it was time for us to launch, we watched a fishing boat venture into the swirling waters. To us it looked as if the boat had hit a brick wall: the water was still flowing too fast and it was forced to retreat. This made us nervous to attempt a launch but, luckily, kayaks were better in rapids than fishing boats, and in any case, we had to make the most of the half an hour of slack water.

We paddled furiously and managed to get through the Yucultas in deceptively innocent looking water. We also had time to negotiate the next set of rapids at Gillard Pass. We almost made it through the third set of rapids but unfortunately time ran out. The water began to increase in speed and we were forced to camp on a small mid-rapid island. Just before we landed another fishing boat veered and listed in front of us, as it struggled to clear the eddying waters at the end of the torrent.

From our island camp we watched with fascination as the rapids developed. It was like a reversible river, raging for six hours in one direction and then six hours in another, with half an hour of comparative stillness in between. At one stage we witnessed a huge bough being sucked under the sea in a whirlpool and erupting violently to the surface some 100 yards down stream.

Day 18 1st May

At first light we were woken by a sharp tapping on the tent pole. In our drowsy state we thought it was an angry farmer hitting the tent

31

with a walking stick. Expecting a right bollocking, for camping on his land, we peered out of the tent to discover that the culprit was a woodpecker! It was still raining and the tide was thundering past the island at a terrific speed. We had to wait until 5pm before we could leave on the slack tide so, to kill time, we made a fire, erected a shelter and ate pancakes. Three resident goats invited themselves to breakfast, and they persistently ate or trod on any food we left unguarded for a few seconds. Even a sharp rap on the nose or a vigorous jab in the rear end with a stick left them undeterred. The futility of our efforts were soon realised, so we resigned ourselves to their company until we left.

At 5pm the tide was still shifting at a fair rate, so we left about 10 minutes later than planned. Once on the water we paddled swiftly down the channel for three miles to a small rocky haven known as Denham Island.

A quick circumnavigation revealed the best landing spot and a good gravel beach to camp on. We both felt exhausted so, after a meal and a warm by the fire, we slid into the tent before it got dark, for some well-deserved sleep. At about 3am Krista nudged me and asked me to listen to the sound of lapping water. I agreed that it did sound close but, in the knowledge that sound always travelled well over water, I dropped off to sleep again. Krista nudged me again and suggested that we should check. I poked my head out of the tent and was horrified to see that the water was only inches away. I looked again at the tide book and only then noticed our error. The tide still had another five feet to rise. In ankle deep water we rapidly uprooted the tent and headed into the safety of the forest to avoid the fast rising tide. Away from the now submerged beach the rest of the island was a mass of large boulders, that made tent pitching impossible. The rest of the night was spent, sandwiched awkwardly between rocks, with the tent propped up over us to keep off the rain.

Day 19 2nd May

Feeling stiff and numb we made a slow start but eventually managed to get ourselves afloat by 10am. We were both tired, irritable and felt totally anti-social. To make things worse it was a cold, miserable day with constant heavy rain interspersed with hail. Despite our moods we still managed to travel 11 miles, mostly against the tide, to the next set of tidal rapids. We stopped early to allow ourselves plenty of time to find a comfortable campsite above the tide line.

The strategy worked and the tent was pitched on a bed of soft pine needles. To catch up on sleep we had an early night to prepare us for the necessary early start, next morning, to catch the rapids at slack water.

Our friendly daily seals watched us prepare for bed and once we had relaxed comfortably into the warm sleeping bags, our tiredness and discontentment of the morning faded into insignificance and we were glad to be here.

Day 20 3rd May

We crawled out of the tent at 5am and, forgoing breakfast, made a good early start. The air was still, with clouds and mist hanging peacefully in the hills. The sun rose gradually from behind the mountains, piercing the cold morning air with its warm rays.

Green Point Rapids proved to be no problem and ten miles further down the channel, we arrived at Whirlpool Rapids, where we ate breakfast. We discovered that missing breakfast was foolish on a trip such as ours, because not only do you feel drained of energy but your body does not get a chance to warm up. It is very noticeable when you spend a long time in the open, how necessary and effective a meal is for sustaining body warmth.

From our breakfast spot at the rapids the view across the channel to the mainland revealed a grotesque example of man's industrial activities. The forest had been razed leaving an ugly scar in place of a lush green area of trees. The scale of this logging scar was fantastic as it stretched for miles along the channel and several miles inland. With timber being a major Canadian export, there must be hundreds of such barren areas in British Columbia. They are, of course, all replanted so that the cycle of growth and logging can begin again.

We caught Whirlpool Rapids at slack tide and passed over them with the minimum of excitement. The afternoon wind whipped up as expected and we slogged against it, passing numerous high waterfalls which cascaded straight into the sea.

We found a good campsite on the mainland, next to a logging scar and adjacent to the main shipping route of Johnstone Strait.

Today had been our longest day so far and, after canoeing 18 miles, we were feeling surprisingly well. Krista caught her first fish and although she was reluctant to kill it, she made a good job of gutting it. My boat developed a hole in the bow, after being dropped on a rock, so we had to tape it as a temporary measure. To make a good fibre glass repair the boat has to be bone dry, so we may have to wait for a sunny spell before being able to effect a more permanent repair. In

33

the meantime, if the need for fibre glassing becomes urgent, it would be possible to make a shelter over the boat, with a tarpaulin, and dry it near the fire.

Oysters had now completely disappeared from the spectrum of sea life and we could only speculate that the water in this area, was either too fast or too cold for them. The distance covered to date is about 200 miles, an average of 10 miles a day.

Day 21 4th May

Most of the day was spent paddling along the main shipping route of Johnstone Strait. It seemed strange to see so many ships after travelling through the relatively unused and sparsely populated channels from Desolation Sound. Tugs, barges, ferries and freight boats all ploughed up and down the Strait linking the remote coastal settlements to the rest of British Columbia. We were now only five miles away from the North shore of Vancouver Island and for much of the day we expected heavy rain and hail from the ominous looking clouds, which drifted towards us from the snowy mountains of the island. Luckily for us they always shed their streaming loads, on the waters of Johnstone Strait, well before reaching us. At the first opportunity we turned off Johnstone Strait into a smaller channel and ended up camping on one of a cluster of tiny islands called the Bocketts. The largest Bockett could be circumnavigated in a few minutes by kayak, and several of the islands housed seal colonies.

The waters proved to be fertile and the fishing so easy that I was able to catch two large cod fish within a minute. With time on our hands in the evening, Krista developed a method of making a cake in a frying pan. Using various types of flour, water, salt, walnuts, raisins, baking powder and sugar, she made a mix of the right consistency and placed it into the cast iron frying pan. This she left near to the fire, rotating it occasionally to heat the cake through evenly. By the end of the evening a perfect-looking, though slightly heavy fruit and nut cake was produced.

Day 22 5th May

We woke to a breezy morning and set off in good spirits towards the town of Minstrel Island. Three yachts glided past under full sail and the occupants of one drew alongside for a chat. They were sailing

34

to Alaska to deliver the boat to a friend, and they expected to be there in four weeks. They laughed when we told them that we expected to be there in four MONTHS! Eight miles short of Minstrel Island we turned into Chatham Channel and were confronted by strong headwinds funnelling through the valley. Progress became slow and our good spirits faded. Even hills in this area seemed oppressive and they had been heavily logged, leaving ugly scars on the once forested slopes. For aesthetic reasons it is now illegal to log closer than a quarter of a mile from the coast of British Columbia but, as far as we could see, this legislation had done little to minimise these man-made eyesores. The timber is exported mainly to Japan, where is it processed and often imported back to Canada and the USA.

Halfway along Chatham Channel we stopped for a break in an attempt to re-coup some strength and enthusiasm, for the remaining four miles to Minstrel Island. For sustenance we cut ourselves a chunk of Krista's cake which proved to be revolting. Unfortunately, some of the flour she had used had gone sour, so with disappointment and still hungry, we paddled on. On our map Minstrel Island was marked as a major town and when we arrived we landed at the floating fuel dock. We had another chat with the yachtsmen and then set off to explore the town. It did not take long because it consisted of one store and one house, but we were able to purchase 4lbs of potatoes, some cooking oil and some stamps. At first we had asked for an aerogramme, but the postmistress had not heard of them. We explained to her what they were, to which she replied, 'What a great idea, it should catch on.' Minstrel Island was linked to the outside world by a weekly sea plane flight which brought mail and supplies. It was still too early in the season for the summer supply boats to arrive, so potatoes were the only vegetables stocked. We soon departed and struck camp on a small island about two miles west of Minstrel Island.

We were ravenously hungry, so we rustled up a large stew which we soon demolished. Still feeling peckish we made some chips, and three pans full saw the end of the potatoes we had intended for the journey. By now I was feeling quite full but Krista evidently was not. She paddled all the way back to Minstrel Island, purchased two more pounds of potatoes, and then proceeded to chip, fry and eat them all. After all that she was still not satisfied and went scavenging for mussels. I was really proud of her! Our food intake had virtually tripled since leaving Vancouver. This is mainly because of the physical energy we were expending every day but also due to the extra energy we needed to stay warm, whilst living constantly in the open air.

Up until now, our route had been running roughly between Vancouver Island and the mainland, but today we started to bear northwards, away from the island, which gave us a definite feeling of progress.

Day 23 6th May

As luck would have it, the sun was shining in the morning so we devoted the day to canoe maintenance. Krista was still ravenous so, before we got down to work, we demolished a breakfast of porridge and pancakes. We fixed new toggles to the ends of our boats to replace the frayed ropes and, using a hacksaw blade as a scraper, I roughened the area around the bow of my boat and left it to dry for a few hours. We were not carrying paint brushes to apply the fibre glass, so we made our own by chewing sticks until the ends frayed. While everything was drying on the beach, we had a wash-and-scrape session in the luxury of pre-heated water.

Krista went to Minstrel Island in the afternoon, for more potatoes and whilst she was away I sat quietly on a rock, splinting our broken spatula together. Suddenly a bald eagle swooped down and landed on the beach some thirty yards away from me. It stood about thirty inches high and its mottled-brown plumage indicated that it was under two years old. Rather like a common sea gull, the size of a juvenile bald eagle is similar to that of an adult and the only obvious differences are the plumage and the apparent lack of fear. The adults usually have black or dark grey plumage with a striking white head, tail and legs. They are also much more wary of humans. The eagle, standing on our beach, had discovered the carcass of a dog-fish and it happily picked at its newly-found treasure. I reached for the camera and managed to stalk up to within about twenty feet of it before it became nervous. I took two pictures and retreated. Its meal was cut short by the rising tide and the remaining bones soon attracted scores of small crabs. In less than an hour the bones had been picked clean, leaving only the skull and gristle.

By the afternoon we had completed the boat repairs and, while the fibre glass dried, we took it in turns to fish from Krista's boat. Fishing was unsuccessful and we both developed backaches. We are hoping that our aches, pains and lack of fitness will improve as the journey progresses.

Day 24 7th May

Plans for an early start were nipped in the bud as from inside the tent the wind sounded ferocious. We set off at about midday and, in-

A Campsite, early in the trip.
Full up and ready to clean the pans

deed, the wind was ferocious. The narrow channel we were in did not have a sufficient catchment area to develop a swell. Instead an aggravating sharp chop hindered progress and, as the day went on, Krista became more and more frustrated and upset. This was not surprising because after a long paddle we only managed eight miles.

There was little wildlife today but, as a consolation, the cloud base was high and we were able to see some magnificent snow-covered peaks. From past experience, I have always found the third and fourth week of any long trip to be the hardest. At this early stage the novelty has worn off, and the destination still seems impossibly distant. We were both feeling the strain and trying, very hard, not to let it rub off on each other.

Our route had taken us down Clio Channel and we camped on an unnamed island at the eastern mouth of Baronet Island. We picked clams for supper and, in the wind and light rain, had great trouble in lighting the essential evening fire.

Day 25 8th May

The wind dropped dramatically during the night, and we woke to a peaceful morning. It stayed clear and calm all day and our morale rose accordingly.

The long channels and large islands that had taken us between the mainland and Vancouver Island, had now broken into a confusion of small, well-spaced islets that reached into Queen Charlotte Sound. The Sound has a reputation, amongst local fishermen, as being a dangerous and volatile sea that is strongly influenced by the Pacific Ocean swells.

Gradually, we emerged from the channel and entered the mass of broken islands, weaving our way northwards. The sea mirrored the rocky islands to perfection and in the sun they looked strangely tropical. Many of the islands were too small to sustain large plants, while others supported twisted, weather-gnarled trees. On some of the larger islands clusters of well-formed, mature spruces had established themselves.

It made a change for us to break away from the confines of the channel and to be able to island hop with the open ocean on one side. It was also delightful to be able to canoe, at a comfortable pace, through peaceful waters, without a head wind to upset us. Today, Queen Charlotte Sound was giving no hint of the nastier side of her character.

Just before landing for the evening we lost both fishing lines. They snagged the bottom, as we drifted with the tide, and could not be retrieved.

Day 26 9th May

In the morning we passed close to a small, thickly vegetated island and, as we cruised by, I caught sight of some large Stella sea lions, basking on a rock, on the opposite side of the island. We landed the kayaks at a safe spot and armed with the camera, we quietly sneaked up on them for a closer look. At first we tried to reach them by a circular route, but found our path ended at a sheer bluff that dropped straight into the sea. We did not want to scare them away or share the water with them if we fell in, so instead, we decided to make our way through the thick vegetation. Drawing nearer, we became concerned with the noise we were making through the alder bushes, so we slackened our pace in order to remain undetected. The loud, deep, snorting and grunting noises grew louder and their sheer size and apparent aggression made us very wary. The bushes gradually thinned and soon we were on open rock, moving very slowly towards the sea lions. A strong odour of rotten fish and blubber pervaded the area. With the combination of their loud barking, their surprisingly large size and our limited knowledge of these creatures, we spent about half an hour creeping stealthily towards them.

Fifteen of them lay on a nearby rock and a huge, scar-covered male shared our island. Confidence came slowly and soon we found ourselves within fifteen feet of the large male. Its sheer size made us feel extremely tense and we were ready to sprint back to the safety of the trees if it turned on us. Adult males attain weights of up to 2,000lbs and, by the size of this harem, we assumed that this male was a mean one! We inched further forward and were soon within ten feet of the beast. The underside of its flippers looked very coarse, rather like the paw of a dog. A four inch scar, on its rump, was of recent origin, showing vividly the rosy pink flesh under the buff coloured fur. As we watched, the females on the other rock began to scuffle amongst themselves, increasing the noise level alarmingly. The extra activity seemed to excite the male and he reared up to get a better view of his harem. Suddenly he noticed us, reared up further and scared the hell out of himself as well as us. With a fearsome roar he launched his huge bulk into the sea, and splashed away leaving us stunned and motionless, with our hearts pumping madly. We made a speedy exit to the safety of the trees and kayaks. Sea lions appear to be very cumbersome on land but, when they put their minds to it, they can move at a remarkable speed on a down gradient. In water their bodies seem to elongate and they glide quickly and gracefully with surprising agility. We spent a couple of hours watching the sea lion colony and it was now time to move on, if we wanted to find a good campsite.

Today had been the first day on the trip that we hadn't seen a single sign of human habitation. Up until now we had always seen either a logging camp, fishing village or fishing vessel during the course of the day.

Krista seems to have lost her appetite!

Day 27 10th May

Although the snow-covered mountains were still visible, Vancouver Island was beginning to look quite distant, as we headed northwards. Storms seem to blow up and subside very quickly in this part of the world, especially at this time of the year. Consequently we had to be on our guard against undertaking any long exposed crossings, in case we got caught out by the unpredictable weather. Breezy areas could be recognised a long way off, on the surface of the sea, as vast dark patches moving across the water. The more defined the contrast on the water surface, the greater the wind difference in the two areas. A sustained wind, as opposed to a squall, we discovered, could often be forecast by an increase in the swell hours before it arrived. Today we had been buffeted by short squalls, but with little likelihood of a sustained wind.

One of the advantages of canoeing this coast line is the choice of routes available. A route could be devised to paddle entirely along the extreme west coast, in waters exposed to the Pacific, or you could opt for a more sedate route in the shelter of the many islands. The section of coast we were on at present, however, was one of two stretches where one has no option but to travel on the extreme west. For the next two days we hoped for good weather to enable us to round the Cape Caution peninsular, to more sheltered waters beyond.

Our food supplies were beginning to run low and we were keeping our fingers crossed that they would last until we reached our first food pick-up point, some 90 miles away, at Bella Bella. Today, to supplement our diet we picked mussels of enormous dimensions. They averaged eight inches long and, because of their size, we could only cook them one at a time. The flesh was rather leathery but tasty and some of them had, what looked like, warts on the flesh. These we ignored until I nearly cracked a tooth on one and discovered they were pearls. The sea was very rich in marine life on this coast line and we noticed that many shellfish grew much larger in areas influenced by a swell.

Day 28 11th May

On studying the charts in the morning, we noticed a village marked on our route, so we decided to make a visit and purchase some food for the next few days. Allison Harbour promised to be a reasonably-sized town so we paddled off towards it. To date, our navigation had been fairly good and we always knew where we were. Today, however, we could not find the town of Allison Harbour. We were positive that we were in the correct area, but obviously something was wrong because the town was not there! After the 37th check of the map, and a double check of the nearby bays and inlets, a fishing boat chugged past. We paddled over to the vessel and asked where Allison Harbour was. 'Allison Harbour', the skipper laughed, 'Hasn't been there for about fifteen years!' The town had been abandoned and totally engulfed by the encroaching rain forest. This sort of navigational error was the result of using charts based on a 1903 survey. The land mass was the same but man-made objects could not be relied upon. By the same token we often came across villages, by surprise, that were not built in 1903. The other navigational hiccup today came when we discovered that we had six miles missing from our charts, so we will have to guess the route until we can establish our position on the next chart.

We made camp on a two mile stretch of golden yellow sand without a footprint on it and the sheer beauty of the beach was a welcome change after the rocky campsites of the last few days. The boat carry was easy because we could drag them up the sand instead of lifting them. We were now poised for Cape Caution and we both hoped that the calm weather would hold out for another day.

Day 29 12th May

The fine, sandy beach of last night did not seem quite so attractive in the morning when we discovered the disadvantages of camping in sand. It gets everywhere; in your hair, your sleeping bag and in your food. After eating our gritty porridge, we had to carefully brush everything before packing it into the boats. Even then a layer of sand managed to settle on the bottom of all our food compartments.

Luckily, the sea had only a small swell so we paddled with ease around the rugged headland, which was adorned with wind-swept trees, and past Cape Caution. We were pleased to get around the Cape with such ease, although in retrospect we found that there were plenty of escape routes available if the weather had turned nasty.

The drizzle of the morning gradually gave way to a lovely sunny afternoon, revealing Vancouver Island, far behind us, for the last time and brightening up the Pacific to the west. The sun felt so warm that we decided to have a much needed, clothes and body wash. Clothes were washed in a trickling stream above the beach and our paddles and tow lines made a good clothes line.

Large mussels were still plentiful so we ate a few six-inchers hoping that they would not be so rich in pearls as the larger ones. Kelp was also plentiful. This long-stemmed brown seaweed attaches itself to the sea bed and grows, in a long, slightly flared tube, to the surface. A bulb-shaped air sac grows at the end of the stem which provides flotation, from which long strips of foliage grow. In this area the kelp grows up to 100 feet in length and is useful to the mariner in several ways. It calms rough water, indicates the direction of the current and a third advantage is that it is edible, cooked or raw.

Our food containers were becoming depleted, so we tried some kelp in the evening stew and were pleasantly surprised at its mild taste.

We had a relaxing evening sitting round the fire and enjoying a picturesque, silhouette view of Egg Island against the open ocean.

Day 30 13th May

Although it rained lightly all day, it was quite pleasant. The sea was very calm and reflected the hills in its greyness. We took advantage of the stable weather and negotiated the two five mile crossings beyond Cape Caution and by the end of the day, we were both pleased that the first set of exposed headlands and crossings were now out of the way.

On a long crossing, constant attention has to be paid to your position in relation to points all around you, to make sure you are not drifting from your proposed goal. Lateral movement, from a distance, can be almost imperceptible, but if a check is made at regular intervals you can determine your drift, and correct your course accordingly. It is just as important to check forward motion, in case you are moving against the current, because it is quite possible to paddle strongly for hours without making progress, if tide abnormalities are not recognised. Most of the time, however, the local tide chart gave us heights and times of tides, and sometimes directions and speeds of currents. Generally in this area the tide floods North and ebbs South, but with the profusion and irregularity of channels, islands and sea depths, the tides often defy all logic. In the case of an inlet, it is fair to assume that the tide floods in and ebbs out, although counter currents also occur around points and in bays.

At this stage, we had not mastered the tides completely and had to execute a three mile ferry glide in order to get to our destination on the other side.

We camped on a white shingle fringed island, savouring the solitude of the fifth day without a sign of land habitation.

The large barnacles and shellfish still fascinated us and it seemed as if we were dwarfs in a land of exaggerated scale! In the water around the island were brightly coloured sea slugs, roughly a foot long and covered with gruesome looking spines about half an inch long. On closer investigation, we discovered that these creatures were similar in substance to starfish, and the dangerous looking spines were soft and jelly-like. They had probably evolved as a devious method of warding off predators. Parts of these slugs are edible but we were not that desperate yet.

Day 31 14th May

We had been very fortunate with the weather just lately and today was no exception. In the afternoon the greyness cleared, and we had marvellous views up the rocky, steep-sided Fitz Hugh Sound for almost forty miles. We were rapidly approaching our first food pick-up at Bella Bella and judging by several ships, in the area, we were now on the main inside passage route northwards. A few passenger ferries passed with people waving, and several slower moving tugs lumbered by, giving us 'toots' of encouragement on their fog horns.

Krista spotted some porpoises and, during the afternoon, we saw about fifteen pairs. They glide and surface gracefully at a leisurely pace, arching their sleek, shining bodies as they come up for air. On a still day like today, you could hear the delicate puff of exhalation each time they surfaced. They were curious about the kayaks but seemed rather timid. We found that if we paddled steadily they would come closer, but as soon as we changed pace or stopped to watch them, they took fright and disappeared.

We noticed that place names on the charts were beginning to sound more Indian than the obviously Anglicised names further south.

Day 32 15th May

We continued up the wide channel of Fitz Hugh Sound towards Namu Village, and again we saw porpoises.

43

Since leaving Vancouver we had been hoping to see whales and were both surprised and disappointed that we had not spotted any by now. Occasionally we saw dark objects surfacing in the distance but they usually turned out to be logs bobbing about on the swell.

The final few miles to Namu were paddled in the company of two bald eagles. They waited high in the trees for us to draw level with them, before flying onward, to the next convenient tree, to resume their vigil. They did not let us out of their sight for about three miles. Close to fishing villages, the eagles associate boats with food, probably because local fishermen clean and gut the fish on deck and throw the entrails overboard, allowing the eagles to feed. Unfortunately, we had nothing to give these magnificent birds and we turned into Namu harbour.

We found Namu Village to be very small. It was constructed on stilts and consisted of concrete buildings and containers that, from a distance, looked more like a space station than a village. Most of the inhabitants of Namu worked in the cannery and lived in cabins near the waters edge. The cabins were connected to each other by raised wooden walk-ways which carried pedestrians over the tangle of lush green undergrowth to the main village area.

The people we met were friendly, particularly the lady in the store, who greeted us warmly with the words, 'Oh, hi, you've made it then!'. We had been spotted three days earlier, by a bush pilot who had landed at Namu for fuel and had spread the word. She even gave Krista a loaf of bread, when we realised that we didn't have enough money to buy one.

We paddled off in a light drizzle and in semi-darkness, set up camp on a crescent-shaped island which had a massive log choke at the end of the beach.

Tides were very high in this area and it was necessary to get the kayaks above the tide line beyond the logs. The steep log choke proved to be an awkward obstacle to negotiate with the boats because not only were the logs large, smooth and precariously balanced, but the boulders on the beach were also huge, slippery and awkward. Carrying the boats was hard enough, but maintaining your own and your partner's balance at the same time, to avoid dropping the kayaks was very difficult. We succeeded after a long exhausting struggle and then settled to a contented evening next to a roaring fire.

Day 33 16th May

In an attempt to make things easier we carried the empty kayaks over the log choke to the sea and then began transporting the camping and cooking gear to the boats for packing. I was by the boats when suddenly I heard the crashing of logs and clattering of pans. I turned to find Krista sprawled motionless over a log. She had obviously taken a heavy fall and the pots, pans and cutlery she had been carrying, were scattered on the rocks. Luckily, she had only winded herself, bruised her ribs and head-butted a log! We dreaded such accidents because emergency services in this part of the world were few and far between, and in the event of a serious injury a long time would elapse before medical help could arrive. Injury had to be avoided at all costs.

Krista recovered quickly, despite a few aching ribs, and within half an hour we were paddling with the tide, towards Bella Bella. We passed a manned lighthouse, which appeared to be far too large for the rock it was built on, and soon landed on a beach some 10 miles from Bella Bella.

Shortly after landing, the 'Love Boat' cruised by, sending up a wake that threatened to damage our kayaks against the rocks on the beach. The crew were oblivious to the concern they were causing us, and they waved an enthusiastic greeting! The 'Love Boat' is the nickname given to luxury cruise ships that regularly plough up and down the inside passages of British Columbia and Alaska.

Day 34 17th May

It was pouring with cold, heavy rain when we got up, and our equipment seemed damper than usual. We paddled towards Bella Bella feeling uncomfortably wet, caused by the water running down the sleeves of our canoeing cagoules.

Our antiquated charts showed Bella Bella in the wrong position and on the opposite side of the channel, was a colourful spread of wooden buildings that we assumed was the New Village. We ignored it and continued round the bend of the channel, away from the obvious town, towards the village marked clearly on our map.

We were both tired and about to turn round when a seaplane spurred us on by landing ahead of us and just round the corner. It had landed in the village of Shearwater, a small settlement named after a bird similar to the albatross. Shearwater was a small fishing and tourist town consisting of a hotel, a post office and a work shed, all housed in one building. We moored alongside the seaplane jetty and made a bee-line for the Post Office, to see if our food packs were there. They were, together with several letters for each of us from home. We were relieved that the food had arrived safely, because without it we would not have been able to continue.

By now it was late afternoon and hunger soon got the better of us, so we piled into the restaurant and ordered a large lunch. The waitress assured us that the 'Fishermen's Dinner' would fill us up, so we ate heartily and washed it all down with a beer. It did not satisfy us and we astonished the waitress by ordering the same again, and eating them just as easily! We decided against a third helping for financial reasons.

Ken, the resort manager, introduced himself to us and explained that he organised sport fishing trips for a variety of rich, international clientele. 'Next week', he told us, 'the third richest man in England is coming to catch salmon with us'. Ken was a strong, friendly character who offered us the use of a caravan, near the seaplane jetty, for as long as we wished to stay in Shearwater. Next door to us another trailer lay on its side in a crumpled heap. It had been wrecked, in 140 mile winds, three weeks earlier. They must have been the same winds we had encountered in the first part of our journey, near Powell River, only we had a milder version.

Our trailer was equipped with a hot shower, a thick carpet to sleep on and a vast area of floor space, which gave us a chance to spread out our equipment to dry.

That evening we met Ken's two fishing guides, John and Kim, in the bar. They were all surprised that we had not seen whales yet. 'Keep your eyes open, they're all over the place, you can't miss 'em.' They also gave us some advice on bears and were even more surprised that we had not seen them yet. 'Why, we see them regularly in the creek just over the channel there.' Kim then boosted our confidence by saying, 'You wouldn't catch me camping in the forest, especially without a gun.' John spoke to us at length about the Queen Charlotte Islands, and suggested that we go there. The Queen Charlottes are a series of remote islands, forty miles off the west coast. A forty mile crossing, for us, was out of the question, but a ferry ran regularly from Prince Rupert, our next food pick-up.

The trailer and the people at Shearwater made our day and we spent a comfortable, cosy night on the carpet listening to the heavy rain drumming on the tin roof. We both slept well, probably because we did not have to listen for animals in the camp.

Day 35   18th May

The rain was still pouring down when we got up, and we were thankful that we did not have to cope with the problems of breaking camp and lighting the fire in the wet. Instead, we treated ourselves to breakfast in the restaurant.

John and Kim, the two fishing guides, noticed that we did not have any fishing gear and to them it was inconceivable to be in Canada without fishing tackle. We explained that we had lost it all in a tide rip, so they took us to their equipment shed and donated a selection of lures, 200 feet of line each and a box of hooks.

Most of the fishermen at Bella Bella were connected with commercial fishing, and there was tremendous rivalry between them and the sports fishermen. The sports fishermen objected to the mass catches of herring, arguing that herring is vital to the sustenance of all sea life, and the way they are being fished at present is upsetting the complex ecosystem of marine life. They also object to the lack of consideration, shown by commercial boats, in the harbour and at sea. After all 'They are all seamen and should know better.'

The commercial fishermen, on the other hand, object to the idea of paying a lot of money for a week's fishing. Catching a few fish seems ridiculous when you can catch plenty of fish and get paid for it. They also react with a degree of jealousy at the way the sports fishing resorts make money for easy work. The disregard for sports fishermen by the commercial fleet manifested itself on the toilet walls of the bar. It read, 'What's the definition of a sports fisherman?' 'A jerk on one end of a line, waiting for a jerk at the other end of the line.'

At midday we collected our food parcels from the Post Office and set about the laborious task of packing the boats. We had 96lbs of food to divide and pack. Luckily, we had the trailer to spread out in, otherwise it would have been very difficult to organise the food on the narrow jetty, in the rain. The hardest thing about dividing the food and packing it was trying to remember who carried what. To avoid repeating the difficulties we had in Vancouver, I carried all the breakfast food and Krista took all the fillers. I took tins of fruit and beans, while Krista took the meats and tinned sweet corn, and so it went on until we reached the stage when we knew roughly who carried what. Everything was placed in two plastic bags to provide a double seal and the packages were then placed in marked plastic ice cream containers for extra security. By evening the rain subsided and we ventured out to pack the boats, ensuring that balance was maintained and every available space was used to the best advantage.

Once the food was in, we packed the tent so that we could get an early start in the morning. As we folded the damp canvas we suddenly noticed that the tent pegs and 'A' pieces were missing. We must have left them at the last campsite some 10 miles back! The thought of paddling twenty miles just to retrieve our tent pegs made us angry with ourselves. Pegs could be easily improvised and so could 'A' pieces with some thought, so before committing ourselves to retracing our route, we asked Ken if we could scrounge around the workshop for suitable metal pipes for replacements. Negative progress was very damaging on morale, but Ken saved the day by saying 'I've got a better idea than that. I'll get one of the lads to drop you at the campsite by boat in the morning. You'll be there and back in half an hour.' We thanked him and went to bed overjoyed at our good fortune, and made the most of another comfortable night in the dry.

Chapter Two: **Whales and Bears, the first sightings**

Day 36 19th May

I dressed warmly and met John on the jetty at 6.30am. He had the boat ready and we sped back to our former campsite where I was hoping to find the pegs. The sea was choppy, but we clipped over the water quickly, avoiding the floating logs that lurked in the dark, choppy waves. He told me that much of the shipping traffic has to stop at night to avoid the log hazard.

In twenty minutes we arrived at the campsite and I leapt ashore whilst John turned the boat. I ran up the beach and crashed through the brush to the cleared spot where our camp had been. There was no immediate sign of the pegs, so I forged my way out again towards the beach. On the way, I was relieved to see the soddon, orange bag lying on a bed of leaves under a moss covered log. They must have fallen without us noticing, as we carried armsful of tentage through the undergrowth. Normally, we double check the campsites but on this occasion we had failed to do so.

The whole recovery operation took less than three quarters of an hour. It would have taken us the whole day in our kayaks. By mid-morning we said our 'goodbyes' and 'thanks' to our friends and, in the rain, began to paddle out of Shearwater. We had only covered about a mile, when a 40 knot wind suddenly blew up. The current was strong, and the waves became irregular and confused. Progress became very slow, and at one point Krista came close to capsizing. We had no choice but to make for a small island which lay ahead. The driving rain and spray had soaked us to the skin, but soon after landing we had a roaring fire going to warm us up.

We had been on the island for about an hour when an Indian commercial fisherman drew alongside to see if we were safe. He had been attracted by smoke coming from the uninhabited island. We told him we were fine and thanked him for his concern. In a shouted conversation he told us that two fishing boats had capsized in the Sound, and he thought the smoke from our fire may have come from the surviving crew members. A few minutes later, a coastguard frigate cruised past and judging by the speed and direction it was travelling, we assumed that the incident had been dealt with. The wind continued to rage throughout the day, so we set up camp and stayed put, amused at only having covered two miles since Shearwater.

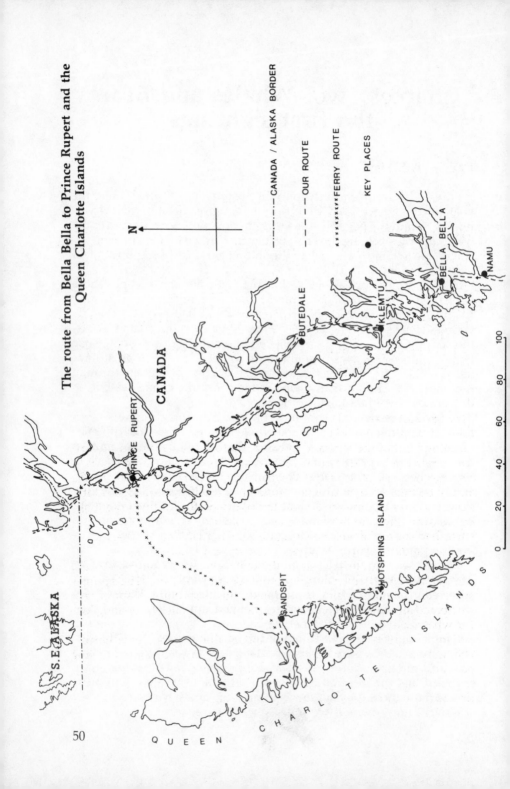

The route from Bella Bella to Prince Rupert and the Queen Charlotte Islands

N

—·—·—·— CANADA / ALASKA BORDER

— — — — OUR ROUTE

×××××××× FERRY ROUTE

● KEY PLACES

CANADA

S.E. ALASKA

PRINCE RUPERT

BUTEDALE

KLEMTU

BELLA BELLA

NAMU

SANDSPIT

HOTSPRING ISLAND

QUEEN CHARLOTTE ISLANDS

0   20   40   60   80   100

The evening cleared slightly and just before dark, a porpoise swam quietly past the island.

Day 37 20th May

The wind abated slightly during the night but the rain continued to bucket down. We canoed, with difficulty, due west along Seaforth Channel into a funnelling ocean swell. The waves broke and pounded against partially submerged rocks, often breaking close to us without warning. Luckily, there was plenty of kelp in the area, so the broken waves maintained little momentum. The wind gradually changed direction during the day, and by the afternoon a very cold, north wind was blowing, bringing with it bitter sheets of hail.

It was too cold to fish, because as soon as we stopped moving, our hands became so numb that they lacked the co-ordination needed for the simple task of reeling in the line.

A rather weak fire did little to thaw us out and we retired early to our damp sleeping bags.

Day 38 21st May

Getting out of the tent and lighting the fire was a real effort today, but a bowl of porridge soon revived us. The day remained wet, in varying degrees of severity. We had hail, drizzle, mist and regular heavy deluges. The sun even shone at one stage, creating a double rainbow close to the sea. To add to the discomfort of this potentially depressing day, the tides were also against us.

Despite the awful weather and tides, we both felt quite cheerful and we saw about twenty porpoises in Matheson Channel.

We also saw whale spumes in the distance and although we could not get close to them, we now knew what to look for. The spumes were very obvious, rising in a dense, bushy cloud of vapour that dissipated after a few seconds. We certainly won't mistake floating logs for whales anymore.

Camp was set up on a small island at the entrance to a narrow channel named Jackson's Passage. Before we landed, John's fishing gear was successfully put to the test to the tune of four rock cod.

The weather cleared in the evening and we were able to partially dry off next to the fire, in the still night air.

We had now covered 408 miles since Vancouver.

Day 39 22nd May

A bright, cheery start to the day took us swiftly with the tide down the hundred metres wide Jackson's Passage. This narrow channel provided the link between two major straits that ran roughly parallel to each other. This enabled us to avoid the fast waters of Heikish Narrows to the North, and at the same time, it took us to Finlayson Channel and the town of Klemtu.

We had travelled three or four miles down the passage, when we realised we had left the fillet knife on the island. The knife was virtually indispensable because, apart from a small pocket knife, it was the only sharp blade we had. Without it we would not be able to prepare the fish. Forgetting the tent pegs was bad enough, but forgetting the knife so soon afterwards was ridiculous! I was very angry with myself and we had to paddle back. I had never experienced such acute annoyance over something as petty as this. To make things worse, as we turned around it began to rain and the wind started up, producing a vigorous headwind. I was so irritated by our stupidity and the negative progress, that I let off steam by paddling aggressively and selfishly ahead, leaving Krista far behind. This was the only time we split up on the trip and I felt guilty at ignoring the basic safety rule of staying together.

Back on the island I discovered that the knife had dropped down between two rocks and was not immediately visible. The day had turned wet and cold and we had already wasted two or three hours of daylight. I was in no mood to carry on so we pitched the tent. Krista went fishing and caught nothing, while I tried to light the fire in torrential rain. Every time a promising flame began to rise, a large drip fell from the tarpaulin and put it out. Each time this happened, the process of making dry wood shavings had to start again. Once the fire was going, we cooked and ate in silence. All in all it had been a thoroughly trying and totally unproductive day, so we had an early night.

Once the damp sleeping bags had warmed up, our moods changed slightly and we discussed the day. In two years, Krista had never seen me angry, and as far as I could remember, I had never felt like that before either. I am usually good at ignoring petty irritations but at this stage of the trip, we were both beginning to notice subtle changes in each other's characters. We would sometimes go quiet, or get annoyed, for little or no apparant cause. The reason, we established, wasn't personal, because we were not getting fed up with each others' company. In fact our feelings for each other remained about the same. the only reasonable explanation was the poor diet and the constant physical exercise. The paddling, in itself, was not too bad, but after nearly six weeks with the combined pressures of carrying heavy boats, keeping dry and warm, camping and only half-sleeping at night was beginning to take its toll. We were also lacking something in our diets. We noted that fats, (an important dietry component when physically exerting oneself and fighting cold for long periods) were virtually non-existant. We were also lacking fresh vegetables and our supply of dried vegetables was only used in small quantities. We could not pin-point our deficiencies exactly, but whatever it was, caused strange quirks in our personalities. In the future we decided to buy plenty of fresh vegetables and drink milk at every opportunity. If we still had the problem when we arrived at Prince Rupert, 170 miles further on, we promised to buy ourselves some vitamin tablets to supplement our diet.

Day 40 23rd May

We woke to the not so unexpected sound of wind and raindrops on the fly sheet. We poked our heads outside to sample the air temperature, but quickly withdrew to the warmth of the sleeping bags. The vote was unanimous, to stay in the tent for a lie-in. The wind and rain continued relentlessly, and we only left the tent when driven out by hunger. The fire started easily and our shelter was surprisingly effective, considering the conditions. We followed our usual pattern for non-paddling days, and settled down to nourish ourselves. Porridge was first, garnished with walnuts and raisins, followed by a two hours feast of pancakes, using lemon, sugar and peanut butter for toppings. Once that was over we rustled up some spaghetti and beans, and retired contentedly back to bed for an early night. Hopefully, the weather will improve tomorrow and we'll be able to make some headway.

Day 41 24th May

I couldn't believe my eyes when I saw that the sun was shining in the morning. We leapt out of the tent, ate breakfast and packed the boats before 9am. While we were packing I discovered a small hole in the underside of my kayak. Sea water had leaked in and caused some food to spoil so I plugged the leak with plumber's tape and hoped it would hold until the next good day.

We were now leaving our food in the kayaks overnight, as opposed to stashing it away from the other equipment. To ensure peace of mind, and to disguise the succulent odour of our food, we rub the cockpits and hatches with mothballs before bed. Apparently, bears do not like mothballs and the smell is so pungent that it masks the more delicate and appealing food smells. The only food kept completely away from the boats and campsite, if at all possible, was fish. Bears are partial to fish, so we always made sure that we washed our hands and the boats after fishing. Disposing of the bones and entrails of the fish after a meal also required some careful thought. They either had to be burned thoroughly, or thrown far enough out to sea so that they would not be washed back on the following tide. A bear's sense of smell, incidentally, is so acute that it can smell food through a tin can.

We paddled off making easy progress through Jackson's Passage but the good weather was punctuated with occasional light showers that created rainbows over the sea. Today was the first time we had seen the mountain peaks for a while, and we were surprised by the amount of snow covering the tops. The snow line had come down to 1,000 feet, which compared with the 2,000 feet snowline at the start of the trip, was quite significant. At the end of Jackson's Passage we crossed the three miles of Finlayson Channel, and headed north towards the small Indian village of Klemtu.

On the way to the village, we stopped to fish, and the water was so clear and calm that we could see the Rock Cod swimming close to the bottom. In quick succession we hooked and landed four of them. It was fascinating to watch them lunging at the lures with their large mouths. They lurk in the rocks on the bottom, moving cautiously and trying not to attract attention to themselves. When potential food swims by they dart out, grab their prey and quickly retreat to the safety of the rocks. These grotesque-looking fish prey on smaller species by swallowing them whole, so that once they snap at a lure, you very rarely lose the fish. In the end I caught a large one, which Krista had spotted in the emerald depths. We let the other four go free, and thrust our quarry into the canvas fish bag.

We pulled into Klemtu Village for supplies and moored to a rickety floating dock alongside a fishing boat. The village consisted of a few dozen wooden houses, clustered around a small wooden church. There were very few people in sight, presumably because they were either in the forest or out fishing. The only noises to be heard were shouts of playing children and a distant chain saw. We walked up the ramp to a stilt platform upon which stood a weathered store. We bought supplies and exchanged stories with the Indian storekeeper before returning to the boats to pack, before the next shower arrived. By the kayaks stood an Indian named Hank, who could not take his eyes off the mysterious, moving canvas bag on my deck. We explained that it was our supper! He was a man of few words but when he did speak, it was very direct. 'Does it always rain like this in Canada?' I asked. 'Yep', 'Even in summer?' 'Yep'. My questions were searching for encouraging signs that might hint at the weather clearing up, but none came. 'Will it get drier in a few months?' I coaxed. 'Nope'. We continued this one-sided conversation for a while, and then he offered to tow us behind his boat. Butedale was the next town on our way and Hank assured us that we would be there by evening, adding that he once rowed it in a day! We chose to camp on a beach approximately one day short of Butedale. It was adjacent to four waterfalls that cascaded, straight down through the trees to the beach. We estimated that the smallest waterfall was 70 feet high, and they all fell within 30 feet of each other.

Day 42 25th May

The day dawned bright and warm so we spent the morning drying out wet clothing and repairing the kayaks. The waterfalls still enchanted us but they were far too icy to risk showering under. There were scores of similar waterfalls in the area, all resulting from heavy snow melts on the peaks. The hills were, on average 3,000 feet high, soaring directly to their summits from sea level and the channels tended to be narrow and straight, creating illusions of never-ending corridors.

With water-tight boats again, we headed northwards up the fjord, refreshed by the sun and relaxed by the activities of the morning.

The water was exceptionally clear on calm days like this and a wide variety of sea life could be seen. Particularly colourful were the starfish and urchins that clung to the rocks, their colours ranging from bright blues to deep reds. We watched some large barnacles feeding, and the feather-like fronds that normally wisp at the water for food, were more like voracious grabbing hands.

By evening we found ourselves paddling against a strong tide so we camped near the end of Sarah Island. Fishing was ridiculously easy. I had always associated fishing with long, boring, uneventful waits, watching floats next to a canal bank, but here we caught four reasonable fish in under ten minutes.

We passed on to our final Canadian chart today and estimated Prince Rupert to be 115 miles ahead and Vancouver 439 miles behind us. The chart was surveyed by Staff Commander D. Pender, R.N., from

1867-1879, and revised in 1907-09. No wonder we have encountered some inaccuracies!

Day 43 26th May

The days were becoming substantially longer, giving us much more time in the evenings for canoeing, and the lighter mornings encouraged us to rise earlier. When we started in Vancouver it was dark by 6pm, but now we could paddle until about 8pm and still allow ourselves an hour of daylight to set up camp.

Today we rose at 6am to catch the tide, only to discover that it was flowing rapidly against us, slowing us down to about one mile an hour. We could not understand why it was flooding south instead of north. By early afternoon the tide was due to ebb, and we expected it to flow in the opposite direction to the flood tide. Instead, it flowed even faster against us! I cannot understand how the tide can flood and ebb in the same direction in a long, narrow channel. Why does it not flood and ebb with us? We had to accept the phenomenon, cast our confusions aside, and settle into a steady pace. We passed many high, spectacular waterfalls and two white water rivers that emptied forcefully into the sea. The snow lay thick on the mountains and on some slopes avalanches had left ragged lines of broken trees in their wake. Today had been the first day without rain for thirty days but it all seemed very worthwhile just to be able to witness this magnificent, natural landscape unimpeded by cloud.

Campsites were difficult to find in this channel because of the steep, rising ground but we eventually found one with a nice rocky perch on which to light a fire. Our evening was interrupted only once when the navy-blue Alaskan State ferry steamed past, sending us scurrying to the boats to get them off the rocks, before the wake hit them. Some of the passengers noticed the fire smoke, and gave us a cheery wave.

We weren't too happy about the tent site for the night. It was reasonably comfortable but there were animal paths running through the trees nearby, and we could not tell whether they were made by deer, bear or wolf.

Day 44 27th May

The wooden buildings of Butedale nestled towards the back of a small bay, beside a thundering waterfall. We moored at one of the two jetties

A long boat carry over slippery rocks

Young bald eagle on a B.C. beach

and walked up the ramp to the shop. In its heyday, Butedale was a cannery and breakdown plant for the fisheries. Nowadays it was more or less a ghost town, with large empty warehouses and disused jetties testifying to its former prosperity. We met 60% of the population; two women and a Norwegian man. The other two inhabitants were away in their boat for the week. We had a cup of coffee with them, and during their friendly small talk, the only thing of interest we learnt, was that one woman hated greasy chips and the other hated burnt ones! They were very surprised that we hadn't seen whales yet, and they gave us a warning about the number of bears in the area.

Butedale runs its own hydro-electric generator from the nearby waterfall, and at night it looks more like downtown New York than a village with a population of five. They need to run the hundreds of lights, to burn up excess energy, and avoid overloading the system!

After a couple of hours with them, they waved us 'good-bye', and we paddled northwards up a long straight channel called Fraser Reach. There was no avoiding the ten miles paddle to the distant headland, because camping in Fraser Reach was impossible. Its craggy, sheer-sided slopes, and lack of landing spots disqualified anyone from camping, unless they had climbing hammocks at their disposal. Our steady pace was broken once, when Krista found a full can of coke floating in the sea. We poured the contents down our throats and continued, reaching the headland at about 7pm.

Almost every day over the past few weeks, we have been hearing a strange sound coming from deep in the forest, but have been unable to pin-point its origin. The sound was rather like a chimpanzee 'hoo-hooing' in the trees. It sounded far too deep for a bird, so we assumed that it must be coming from a larger animal. Whenever we heard the noise, we tried to avoid camping nearby in case it came to investigate us. The sound had caused us several sleepless nights, and this evening, as we ate our meal next to the fire, the deep 'hoo-hoo' sound started up, very close to us. We huddled nearer to the fire, and tossed on another log for safety. There was not much else we could do, because the creature was far too close. Suddenly it came into the light of the fire and horror of horrors, it was a grouse! The sound that had caused us so much concern turned out to be the seasonal mating call of a harmless, male game bird.

Just recently Krista's wrists have swollen slightly, and were causing us both some anxiety. We will have to take it easy for a while to avoid the disaster of a serious strain.

Day 45 28th May

Krista found a tin of Swiss coffee washed up on the beach and we sampled it at breakfast time.

The morning was strangely silent and misty, with visibility limited to a few yards along the beach.

The sound of an approaching boat engine pierced the stillness, and it seemed to take ages before it came into view through the mist. It was moving very slowly, closely hugging the coast on our side of the channel. The skipper saw our fire and slowed down. All on board were local Indians, who enquired, over the 'hum' of the engine, about our well-being. Glad of their concern for us, we thanked them for looking in, and watched their cheerful waving forms fade into the mist.

On perfectly flat water we paddled to Nelly Point on Whale Channel. We couldn't see the other side, so we set the compass and travelled on a strict bearing, aiming slightly south to counteract the drift. Whale Channel is three miles across, and within a few minutes of leaving the shore we could not see anything in any direction, apart from mirror-grey water, mist and the occasional floating log. Halfway across we went through a school of porpoises, whose black, shiny skins appeared like razor-sharp silhouettes against the white, moist background. Two of them swam so close to the boats that it was possible to see their six-foot forms darting about beneath us.

We knew the end of the crossing was near, when the mist ahead began to appear slightly darker, than in other other directions. Soon beaches and trees came into focus and we knew we were near to our destination on Gil Island.

Krista caught a large rock fish and tied it to her deck, with a tow line, while I rushed over with the fish bag. In the sea, Rock fish protect themselves, either by wedging themselves between rocks with their spines, or by making themselves look large by fanning out all their fins. This natural reaction provided us with plenty of handy protrusions, making them easy to tie on to a boat. As soon as Rock Cod are hooked, they rarely fight like other fish. Instead they fan out and, in this immobile state, they are very easy to haul aboard.

In the evening we watched porpoises swimming close to the island and occasionally, we caught glimpses of leaping salmon that had arrived prematurely for the annual Pacific salmon runs.

Day 46 29th May

We decided early in the day, to have a leisurely paddle to give Krista's wrists a chance to recover. Luckily for us it was a calm day, so we started the three miles crossing of Wright Sound with great enthusiasm. Halfway across we noticed some large, white splashes ahead of us. We estimated that the splashes were about one and a half miles away, but we could not tell exactly what was causing them. Judging by the size, we guessed they must be whales and excitedly, we stroked towards them keeping our eyes on the distant movements. About a mile short of our goal, the splashing stopped, so we slowed down and resigned ourselves to the anti-climax of losing them. Moments later we were surprised by a 'whooshing' noise behind my boat. I turned just in time to see the six-foot dorsal fin of a 'Killer' whale, knifing through the water with startling speed towards me. It submerged about forty feet away from us and swam straight underneath our kayaks. Soon another broke the suface near us, with a sudden puff and its body surged through the water like a surfaced submarine, before gliding into the depths, with its huge fin sinking out of sight last of all. Soon others came and, after a minute or so, we counted four of them, circling and puffing close to the boats. We rafted together and ate some cake whilst we watched them dive and swirl around us. The noise, power and speed of them, reminded me of an express train. It was an unnerving experience having killer whales darting about under the kayaks for the first time, but it was a superb feeling to be so close to such impressive animals in the wild.

The killer whale is one of the few species of 'toothed' whales, and is a remarkably efficient predator. They hunt and eat anything catchable, such as fish, squid, seals, sea lions, sea birds, and have also been known to attack larger whales, who are defenceless against 'wolf-pack' tactics. No accounts have been reported of humans being eaten by them, but we thought it would be unwise to give them the opportunity! There have been reports of sailing boats being attacked by them, but these dubious and isolated occurences, have all taken place in the open ocean.

The correct, and less misleading, name given to this large, propoise-like whale is the Orca (orcinus rectipinna). Males grow up to thirty feet long and females about twenty-six feet. They are mostly black, with white eye patches, bellies and flanks. Close up, they look extremely clean and powerful and although it is one of the smaller species of whale they look extraordinarily large!

The dorsal fins grow up to six feet in males, and are long, pointed and triangular in shape. Individuals can be identified by the size and shape of this fin.

We were surprised at the speed they travelled under water, and found out later that they are the fastest marine animal, capable of cruising at thirty knots. They swam around us on this occasion, for about five minutes before disappearing under the sea and re-emerging over a mile further on. The speed they must have swum to attain that distance was inconceivable.

Like the dolphin, the orca is extremely sensitive and intelligent. One of the fishermen at Bella Bella told us that one day, the entire Bella Bella fishing fleet was out fishing in a confined channel. The commercial and sports fishermen all had their nets and lines cast when a pod of twenty or so orcas appeared. They approached the fleet rapidly and dived under the boats before the fishermen had time to pull up their lines. Shortly afterwards every single whale emerged beyond the fleet, without so much as even brushing a line or net. He summed up the story of killer whales with these words, 'Don't worry about their name, they're just big, soft dolphins.'

Even so, when you are sitting in a small kayak, bobbing like a cork on the ocean with 1,500 feet of dark water beneath you, you feel very vulnerable and insignificant when you know that these huge, powerful creatures are lurking below.

We paddled slowly on, jabbering excitedly to each other, about the thrilling events of the afternoon.

Fishing was poor today although Krista did hook a huge blue-green Sunstar. Sunstars have dozens of thick tentacles, radiating from a flat, circular body, hence the name. They are one of the largest starfish in the world.

Day 47 30th May

We made a damp start in the morning, but a good tidal current zipped us about 15 miles up Grenville Channel, before it changed direction and created difficulties for the next five miles. We camped on a stony beach, at a point where the long, straight, narrow channel flared slightly.

I lost two jigs whilst fishing in the current. Fish bite more frequently in moving water, but unfortunately the hooks tend to snag on the bottom more often. Krista's wrists were still playing up, but with Prince Rupert only 45 miles away, we shall rest there for a couple of days.

Day 48 31st May

Using the tides as an excuse, we treated ourselves to a lie in, and spent the rest of the morning eating pancakes. Later in the day we put eight miles behind us, ending up at a small bay opposite Baker Inlet where Krista caught two of the largest rock fish we have ever hooked. They were so much easier to gut than the small, fiddly ones and they did not fall apart when we cooked them.

We are both looking forward to leaving Grenville Channel tomorrow. Psychologically, it is much harder to travel down a long channel, than it is to island hop and progress feels very slow when you are confined between two parallels because you aim at the same landmarks you were paddling towards the day before.

Day 49 1st June

The tide in the morning was exceptionally low, and it revealed a daunting obstacle course of steep, seaweed-covered rock. We used logs to make a trackway and once they were sited to our satisfaction, we slid the boats one at a time, over the smooth wooden trail to the water.

There was a slight chop on the sea, and we noted that the water had changed colour from clear blue to murky brown. We were still about 30 miles from the mouth of the Skeena River, but the silt transported from the interior was already evident in the sea.

At about midday, over the sound of the lapping waves, Krista shouted, 'We haven't seen whales for ages.' Immediately, as if in response to her comment, there was a puff next to her boat and a whale surfaced! It followed us for about half an hour, swimming and diving alongside for short periods, puffing each time it rose to the surface. It was moving slowly and gracefully at our speed, sometimes dropping back a little and sometimes surfacing in front. It gave us the impression that it wanted company on its journey and we were pleased to have it with us for a few miles. It looked much more gentle than the orca and swam with much less urgency and aggression. It finally left us when the silt thickened and retraced its route back into Grenville Channel.

It had been a Minke whale, otherwise known as the Pike, or sharpnose finner. Minkes are another of the smaller species of whale, attaining a maximum length of 30 feet. They nearly always travel alone and often follow boats, particulary those under sail. Its most distinguishing features were its small dorsal fin located near the tail, and the habit of keeping its tail flukes below the sea, even when diving. Once it even lifted its jaw clear of the water, revealing the deep grooves of its throat and the fibrous mouth lining. Minke are baleen whales, or filter feeders, and perhaps their feeding habits explain the differences

The stilted store at Klemtu

A Grey Whale in Canada

between the swimming and travelling styles of the baleen and toothed whales, ie speed and power are not essential for a non-predator.

Towards the end of the day, we were crossing the mouth of a large bay, when I noticed a small, black speck moving along the beach. We were too far away to see exactly what it was, but by the comparative size of the logs nearby we guessed that it was a bear. It was the first we had seen so we paddled excitedly towards it. The bear sat non-chantly in the lush, green grass next to a stream. It was a black bear, much smaller than the brown or grizzly, but just as worthy of respect. We were downwind and managed to get within about fifty yards of the animal. They are short-sighted creatures and even though we were sitting in brightly-coloured crafts, it could not see us. We edged closer and closer and after a few minutes were near enough to hear it munching the grass. It was still not aware of our presence, although it did occasionally sniff the air, as if catching a brief waft of our scent.

Fascinated, we sat and watched for about forty five minutes, keeping a wary eye open for a second bear in the forest. Although close to the shore, we felt quite secure in the knowledge that if one charged us, we would be able to make a speedy retreat in our kayaks. Not knowing anything abouth their behaviour, we didn't want to take any chances.

Our viewing of this strong but docile-looking animal came to an end when it started to rain. The bear raised itself from the sitting position on to all fours and sauntered off into the trees for shelter.

We were surprised at the size of the black bear and now we had actually seen one in the wild, it reinforced the importance of careful camping.

On the beach campsite that evening, we were treated to a high diving display by an over zealous kingfisher, and a family of sea otters also kept us company.

Day 50 2nd June

The boat carry in the morning was exceptionally easy. All we had to do was to ski them over the slimy surface of the beach to the water. The mouth of Skeena River was still fifteen miles away, but its influence was strongly evident. Apart from the obvious discolouration of the sea, the currents were notably stronger and the directions unpredictable, particuarly where the tides met the river waters head on.

On the crossing to Dehorsey Island the sea kept us on our toes, with ever-changing currents and back-washes. We avoided the obvious areas of confused water by continuously changing course and re-assessing the currents as they altered with the incoming tide. Definite lines could be seen stretching erratically in various directions across the channels, indicating the meeting of waters of different origins and speeds. Within two miles, the water changed direction five or six times, threatening to drag us off course, into dangerous looking waters.

Once the crossing was over, we felt reasonably safe and were able to hug the coast and escape the moving water. We paddled through the thick, chocolate-brown sea, in the company of a dozen or so seals and sea otters, to a campsite about a day's journey from Prince Rupert. Camp was on Inverness Passage, in sight of the mainland, and well past the main veins of the Skeena River delta.

Civilisation was obviously close at hand, because numerous wooden boat wrecks lay decaying in the mud on both sides of the passage. We had also passed two disused canneries and the concrete remains of Second World War gun emplacements. The main item, that confirmed our imminent contact with civilisation however, was the sighting of a car, the first seen for 38 days!

Just before dark, a goods train hauling ninety-nine carriages, rumbled by on the opposite bank, and the driver greeted us with a wave and a long blast on his horn. We shared the tent with numerous mosquitoes but despite this, we were pleased that we were within striking distance of Prince Rupert.

Day 51 3rd June

Krista woke up feeling aggravated but as usual, we could not put our finger on what was wrong. We assumed it was the effect of an exhausting trip with little fresh food.

It was a cold, damp day, and at low tide, it was difficult to distinguish between mud and water. The first hour was consequently spent trying to choose the best course through a maze of dead ends, mud banks and channels until the tide level rose.

At one point, we saw a bald eagle swoop out of the sky, with its talons open, and pluck a small stranded flounder from the muddy bank. The luckless fish did not stand a chance against such speed and accuracy. The talons of the bald eagle are razor sharp, with a tight curve, designed for perfect gripping. When used to grip a fish of the right size and weight, they are uncompromisingly effective, but once it latches on to a large fish, it cannot release its talons until it lands. The hooked shape, combined with the hanging weight, makes release nearly impossible in the air or water. Eagles have been observed to get dragged underwater by a prey too large to control and one fisherman we met had witnessed an eagle drowning when it had been unable to release a large salmon.

Bald eagles can swim, but have great difficulty in taking off from the water with wet feathers. For this reason most of their fish are caught near the surface with precision flying.

We continued through the silty water, passing large steel coal-landing constructions, canneries, factories and fishing boat jetties until, finally, we were paddling parallel to Prince Rupert's waterfront.

A Japanese boat was busily loading timber from a vast floating log-boom and all along the waterfront commercial fishing vessels chugged back and forth. One fisherman shouted words to the effect that we were nuts and suggested that we take the ferry.

The actual town centre was easy to recognise by the collection of modern concrete buildings, whereas the residential area was spread up the side of the darkly forested mountain. Corrugated steel warehouses lined the shoreline, which was fringed by moored fishing boats and fuel jetties.

We paddled the entire length of the Prince Rupert waterfront and moored in the pleasure boat dock. We had to land there, because most commercial fishing bays only allowed landing access to craft connected with their particular cannery.

Uncertain of what to do next, we decided to search for a café so that we could dry off. Being a Sunday, the Post Office and most shops were closed, so drinking tea seemed to be the best plan to start with. It was raining hard so we quickly tied the boats up and secured the tarpaulin over the cockpits.

As we left the jetty, Alex Murdoch made himself known. He worked for the Forestry Commission in Prince Rupert and when he heard that we only just arrived, he gave us a tour of the town in his car. Prince Rupert stretches for about 10 miles along the north west coast of Kaen Island, overlooking the dark waters of Prince Rupert Sound. Its large area was unusual for a coastal town in this area and its size was attributed to the fact that it was linked to other parts of British Columbia by road, rail and sea. Most other towns are served only by sea and air.

Alex dropped us at a café near the harbour and we sat conspicuously damp and scruffy, amongst the other customers. It is only when you are suddenly thrust from the wilds into a civilised situation, that you realise how rough you really look! Halfway through our burger, Alex re-appeared and invited us to stay at his house. The thought of a warm, dry bed, a hot shower and an evening free of animal noises influenced

66

the decision and we eagerly accepted. Alex was in his mid-thirties with two teenage children and a kind wife. They were a mine of information about the wildlife, forestry and local history and they had done a few adventurous sailing trips up and down the coast. As with the fishermen at Bella Bella, they recommended a visit to the Queen Charlotte Islands and because of them we decided to embark on a two week canoeing holiday straight from Prince Rupert.

The Charlottes lay forty miles west across the volatile Hecate Strait, and stretch in a north to south direction, for some 200 miles in an archipelago of rugged islands.

The evening shower felt good and we even washed and dried our clothes before enjoying warm beds in a friendly environment.

Day 52   4th June

It had been a very pleasant night, with no sticks, pine cones or boulders to contend with.

We spent most of the day in town visiting banks, shops cafés and most importantly, the Post Office to confirm that our food packages had arrived safely.

The town of Prince Rupert acquired its unusual name after the Grand Trunk Pacific Railway organised a national competition to find a suitable name for British Columbia's newest and most northerly port. The only stipulation was that the name should not have more than eleven letters. A lady from Winnipeg won the first prize of 250 dollars, but there was such an uproar over the fact that the winning name had twelve letters, that the organisers had to chose a second winner to receive the same amount.

Prince Rupert was the first Governor of the pioneering Hudson Bay Company, and was also the grandson of King James the First. He had a distinguished record in European campaigns and he fought in the English Civil War, as head of the Royalist forces.

In the evening Krista and I snapped ourselves back to reality by watching 'Indiana Jones' at the cinema.

Chapter Three: Holiday in the 'Charlottes'

Day 53 5th June

Alex dropped us off near the harbour and bade us farewell. With renewed vigour, after such a comfortable day off, we sprang into the kayaks and paddled to the ferry terminal. We opted to travel to the Queen Charlotte Islands the easy way, rather than risk a 40 mile paddle across Hecate Strait. At the terminal the crew helped us load our heavy, vegetable-filled kayaks, before allowing the other passengers to embark.

The ferry cast off and retraced our earlier route, past the railway lines and jetties before heading west through some unfamiliar islands to the open sea.

The actual crossing was rather sedate and uneventful because there were very few passengers on board, very little to look at and the sea was calm.

Two major islands make up the Queen Charlotte chain, with other smaller islands dotted around close by. Graham Island was the most northerly of the two large islands and judging by the map, was rather flat with long stretches of beach line. Moresby Island looked much more interesting, with numerous irregular inlets, peninsulars and islands. The topography of the island looked more impressive as well, with mountains stretching high above the snow line.

As we approached the Charlottes our observations proved to be accurate. The flatness of Graham Island looked uninviting to us, and the sight of those distant southerly mountains confirmed that we had made a wise decision to head southwards to Hot Spring Island.

The ferry docked at 5pm at Skidegate and we struggled off with our boats. The chief crew member described them as, 'the heaviest Goddam kayaks' he had ever lifted.

Before leaving the village of Skidegate, to search for a campsite, we met a goatherd from Greenland, who told us about some deserted Haida Indian villages 30 miles further south. He marked our maps for us and we decided that we would try and find them.

Day 54 6th June

It was a beautiful, clear, sunny day and we paddled across Skidegate Inlet toward the town of Sandspit. Near the end of the crossing, Krista spotted some large splashes beyond the town, amongst the low tide sand bars. The splashes rose again and again and, because of their size, we knew it could not be a whale's spume. They were obviously being caused by a heavy object landing in the sea, possibly a whale leaping. We paddled out through the maze of sand bars to investigate, keeping our eyes glued to the area where the splashes had occurred. As we closed in, the splashes ceased and in their place we began to see the occasional vaporous spume. Adjacent to a steeply shelved pebble bank, we caught sight of two fins above water. They were about three feet high and cut through the water like the dorsal fin of a shark. The fins looked menacing, so we gave them a wide berth and landed on a gravel bank. When we approached on foot, the creatures disappeared into the deep water, and a few moments later they surfaced, puffing their spray loudly into the air. We were relieved to know that we had been sharing the water with grey whales and not sharks. The confusion had arisen because when we first saw them, they were swimming on their sides and their tail flukes projected out of the water, looking like shark fins. Most whales have no dorsal fins and if they do, they are usually very small and indistinctive. The only shark in these waters that can compare in size with a whale, is the basking shark. They can attain lengths of forty feet or more but despite their enormous dimensions, they are filter feeders and pose no threat to small craft. The only possible danger from a basking shark can come from an accidental swish of its tail.

The 'Greys' and the fishermen of the Queen Charlottes do not get along very well because the whales often get caught in fishermen's nets, causing damage of up to $4,000 per net. Tragically for the whales, entanglement in nets usually means death by drowning and because of this, the fishermen try to ward off the whales by shooting into the water close by. If that fails they shoot the whale to avoid damage to their nets.

An incident involving the Skidegate fishermen was described in the local newpaper. They were shooting around a whale to frighten it away from their nets and the museum curator, who did not agree with their methods, recorded the incident on a video camera. The hereditary chief who spotted him with the camera, beat him up and destroyed the film. The chief then had a heated argument with the curator's wife and, while this was going on, someone threw a seal bomb. The wife and the chief fled in panic, thinking the other side was sniping at them.

69

In the end the curator and his wife left town, and stayed away for a month before they dared to return. The newspaper report went on to describe the despicable actions of native Indian terrorists who had resorted to throwing bombs. What actually happened was that one of the young fishermen, for a joke, had let off a seal bomb to stir things up. (Seal bombs are used for stunning seals and are otherwise harmless.) The whole fiasco, despite being vaguely amusing, underlined the strength of feeling running on both sides. The fishermen were aware of the adverse publicity a whale shoot would attract, and the curator was obviously aware of the reaction of the fishermen if he were caught photographing them. There are, of course, two sides to the argument and it all boils down to the conflicting ideals of conservation against livelihood.

Our camp in the evening was on a grey, sandy beach, which had some disturbing animal tracks running along its length. They were large, well-spaced and made by a heavy animal. The 'pan' shaped track was not very distinctive in the dry sand, but some prints were doubled up, suggesting a four-legged creature. It was far too late to move on that night, so we camped anyway and lit a hugh fire for peace of mind.

Day 55 7th June

During breakfast we discovered that the foot prints of the previous night had been made by a horse.

Amused by our paranoid fear, we relaxed a little and set off, only to discover after a few hundred yards, a bear ambling over the rocks. The sight of it was a surprise but it reassured us that our fears were not entirely unjustified. Bears come down to the sea at this time of the year, to eat the lush spring grass that grows abundantly at the forest edge.

Shortly before their winter hibernation, bears change their diet and concentrate on eating bark, pine needles and small twigs. This passes through their alimentary canals and eventually lodges in the form of a bung in their rectums. This prevents the creatures from soiling their dens during hibernation. With the advent of spring, the bears emerge from their dens and their most pressing priority is to get rid of the bung. To do this they eat roughage, in the form of spring grass, and this soon clears the tubes. For this reason, bears tend to be a little moody early in the season.

The wind blew up before lunch and the tide flowed strongly against us. The going was difficult but we were amply compensated by clear skies and magnificent views. Two sea lions followed us for a few miles and there were many eagles and seals about, to take our minds off the slog.

Our water supply was very low and the availability of running water was paramount in our search for a campsite. The main problem was that all the streams were concealed beneath the stony beaches or obscured by the dense forest. In the end our struggle against the wind became too much, so we landed regardless of our water shortage and to our surprise, a tiny stream gurgled invisibly beneath the pebbles at our feet.

The evening was pleasant so we took ourselves for a stroll along the beach to stretch our legs. To ease the trudge of walking on pebbles, we leapt from log to log along the bleached choke of driftwood which had been washed to the head of the beach by past storms. It was very quiet, apart from the scurrying sound of hundreds of crabs that took refuge as we passed above them.

Suddenly, through the stillness, we became aware that the trees were rustling behind us. We both felt nervous. Something was hiding in the trees nearby, so trying not to feel too jumpy, we turned around and walked back to the camp. It was late when we arrived back at the site, so we dowsed the fire and walked through the bushes to the tent. To our horror the tent had been severely bent. Obviously something heavy had leaned on it, making the previously straight, ridge pole 'U' shaped. A tooth hole and a slobber mark were on the fly sheet, confirming our suspicions of what had caused the damage. It was almost dark by now and the option of moving camp would have been foolhardy with these tides. The only practical solutions were to frighten the bear by making loud noises with our pots and pans, and to light a large, smoky fire at the mouth of the tent.

In the dark we retired nervously, and reluctantly crawled into our sleeping bags, knowing that there was a curious bear very nearby.

Day 56 8th June

It was sheer relief to see the morning arrive after such a sleepless night but one advantage of the incident, was that it gave us the incentive to get up early. It was another sunny day and as soon as breakfast was eaten and the ridge pole straightened, we headed south on the outside of Louise Island to the the deserted Indian village of Skedans. It made a change to be paddling south instead of north, but the main disadvantage was the sun. In the northern hemisphere it travels south

What happened when a bear leaned on the tent

Two purple hinged scallops enjoy a bath on Hotspring Island

in the sky, so on clear days we were dazzled for the whole day.

The forest had done a good job of concealing Skedans village and, disappointed at our failure to find it, we paddled into Skedans Bay, a shallow cove of clear water, bordered by a sandy beach. Halfway across the bay, Krista shouted, 'A whale! Over there!'. Sure enough there was a spume of vapour hanging over the sea. We paddled towards it for a closer look, and in the clear green water it was possible to see the shape of a whale under the surface. We followed it for a while and soon realised that it was swimming backwards and forwards in the same area, surfacing every 100 metres or so for three or four breaths. It was another Grey Whale, about 30 feet long, and apparently at home in our presence. We paddled as close as possible to it and watched its large, pale form move slowly under the water. It soon became curious about us and started swimming under our boats to get a better view. The first time it cruised under the kayaks, Krista turned to me and said, 'Now this is frightening!' We spent about two hours with the whale, catching glimpses of its disproportionately small eye, as it swam underneath on its side.

It was an extremely graceful swimmer. At first the knobbly mound of its blow hole would break the surface with a cloud of vapour. As it dived again the blow hole would submerge, followed by the curved back and tail, all following through in a continuous, serpent-like motion. The movement was always completed by the tail flukes lifting clear of the water and sinking slowly from view into the sea.

As the afternoon progressed, the tide came in and the whale stopped ploughing up and down the bay. Instead, in the now deeper water, it started some more localised activities. It began by blowing bubbles under the water making the water 'boil', then surfacing violently through the bubbles with its jaws agape, as if snapping at the air with its mouth. This looked a little dangerous to get too close to, so we observed from a distance. The head was covered in crusty barnacles set around a coarse, furry mouth, the appearance of which was not in keeping with the grace we had witnessed earlier.

The afternoon had been fascinating and as we turned to leave, the whale swam quickly towards us, with the white shadow of its body aimed directly at Krista's boat. It was surfacing and looked as though it was going to come up right under her canoe. I was certain she would be lifted out of the sea so, thinking that an airborne kayak would make a good shot, I shouted, 'Take a photo!'. She told me to visit a taxidermist and at that moment, the whale surfaced with its blow hole only a foot from Krista's boat. It dived again and I was convinced that she would be knocked in by the tail. To our surprise, it brushed its way gently under her boat without even nudging it. Up until then we hadn't seen the whale dive without raising its tail flukes and we left, marvelling at the sensitivity of the creature.

In the forest behind our campsite, the ground was littered with abalone shells, dropped from the tree tops by eagles who had feasted on the flesh inside.

Day 57 9th June

Good weather helped us paddle steadily for about twenty miles, to a broad, sandy beach on Lyell Island. The water was clear and, apart from occasional stretches, we could see the sea bed for most of the way.

Porpoises followed us for a while at a 'safe' distance, and the air was so still that you could hear their whispery puffs as they surfaced.

We caught five fish for tea and developed a new way of skinning the raw fish. You simply hold a flap of skin, near the head end of the fillet, and cut with a sharp blade between the skin and the flesh. The flesh hangs down and the weight of the meat virtually peels it from the skin.

Our two recent 'bear' incidents had an effect on us this evening and we both found ourselves running scared from our own footprints in the sand.

Day 58 10th June

At 6.30am it promised to be another bright day, but by 8.30am, when we emerged from the tent, the weather had changed dramatically. It had clouded over and the wind was whistling but we only had a five mile paddle so we left, and aimed for Hotspring Island.

Hotspring Island was small enough to walk around in fifteen minutes but, despite its small size, it played host to an impressive forest of giant spruce trees, the largest we had seen on the coast so far.

We secured the boats on the beach and, armed with a towel, walked through the forest in search of the hot springs. The shore on the opposite side of the island was more rugged than where we had landed, but there was no sign of a hot spring. We turned and walked back along the beach toward the boats when suddenly, behind a rocky outcrop, we saw people. We had not seen a soul for five days and to encounter a whole group of them was quite unexpected. There was a small cabin, partially obscured by lines of laundry, and near the cabin was a steaming pool of natural hot water, in which sat a dozen or so raucous lumberjacks. They were laughing, shouting and drinking beer from a crate that stood on a piece of floating wood. Pleased to have found the spring, we stripped off and jumped in for a welcome dip. The loggers were from a forestry camp on Lyell Island, and this was the way they spent their rest days. They were a loud, boisterous crowd who introduced themselves as 'the ones responsible for the rape of the landscape around here'. One added, in a loud voice, 'Yeah, at least you can see the hills now. Brown stumps are much nicer than green trees, I think.'

Unfortunately, we had missed most of the party and the crates were virtually devoid of beer. Their foreman was having a hard time trying to persuade the men to leave the pool before their launch became grounded by the tide. The men did not want to budge and a verbal battle began to rage around us, between the foreman and the men in the bath.

As they fought it out, one of the loggers told us a story about the time a boat load of school girls arrived on a field trip from Vancouver. He explained that the girls were rather snooty and the teacher was a real bitch. She was about 99 years old and protected the girls like a mother hen. He went on, 'Anyway, all us boys arrived and jumped in, stark naked, whooping and hollering in the middle of this crowd of shrieking girls. Gave them the shock of their lives! The teacher nearly had heart failure and ushered her girls to safety. Wow, that was a day. We never did see them again.'

One by one the loggers succumbed to the foreman's threats, and sauntered towards their waiting boat.

Also sharing the island with us, was a team of ornithologists, who were primarily studying the Hooded Murelets. They were living in the cabin and their serious dedication to their work contrasted extraordinarily with the personalities of the loggers. They supplied us with fresh water and fed us with pancakes, while they explained in detail the nesting and breeding cycle of the murelet. They also gave us a series of bird impressions to enable us to recognise other species. We left the hut in the evening totally confused and with our heads ringing with bird songs.

Day 59 11th June

When we got up in the morning we decided to devote the day to maintenance tasks. I mended a leak in Krista's boat while she patched the badly rotted tent bag and replaced the toggles on each end of the kayaks. I then sewed the waterproof skerry bag together, while Kris did battle with the neoprene cuff of my sea cagoule. Once the chores were completed we had a second breakfast in the company of the bird-watchers. They quizzed us about the birds we had spotted near our campsite and again we left them with our heads resounding with various whistles and chirps. They were amazed at our complete ignorance of North American birds and were openly shocked when Krista announced, 'They all look like ducks to me!'

A short scramble over the rocks revealed more warm pools. Altogether there were three, plus a hut containing three hot baths and an old tin bath on the beach. The tin bath was by far our favourite. It was sited in the middle of a wind-swept beach, only a few feet from the waters edge. Leading to the bath were two plastic pipes, one for hot and the other for cold water. Temperature adjustment was effected by flicking the appropriate pipe out of the way with your toes. We treated ourselves to a long soak and it was a wonderful feeling lying on a wind-swept beach, in a hot bath, with waves breaking on the shore and eagles soaring overhead.

On our way back to camp we met Rob and Kevin, two kayakers on a week's holiday. They had been dropped off on Hotspring Island the previous evening and planned to canoe to a salmon hatchery several miles north. They greeted us with a jovial, 'Are you the Limeys?' I replied, 'Give us a swig of that whisky and I'll tell you.' They were a comical pair who had never kayaked before. One described himself as a 'biological trouble-shooter, specialising in sprats'. The other sold money to people. We were all going roughly in the same direction, so we decided to loosely travel and camp together. This, they joked, was a good idea, as it meant there was only a 25% chance of being eaten by a bear, instead of 50%. We helped to lighten their load by sampling their whisky and biscuits, whilst they devoured our pancakes and popcorn. Later in the evening we had another bath, whilst our friends went on a practice paddle round the island. When they got back, we were stunned to hear that they had set a crab trap by using steak as bait!

We passed the evening round the fire, laughing and swapping unlikely stories. To date it had been impossible to have a social life and this change of company was a real tonic for us. Although we enjoy each others company, after fifty nine days, the chance to laugh and chat with a couple of fresh personalities improved our morale no end. We retired to bed refreshed and in high spirits.

Day 60 12th June

At about 10am we paddled through a light mist to the opposite side of Hotspring Island where Rob and Kevin were still packing equipment into their kayaks. This was the first time they had packed the boats and it reminded us of our first attempts. To make more room we carried some items for them and they donated their crab trap to us, declaring that it was useless, and a waste of steak! They laughed continuously at their efforts, in a situation where lesser mortals would have been kicking the boat. Once they had launched, we consulted the chart and agreed on a campsite. We paddled the first three miles of open water together and then they steamed off up the channel, ahead of us and out of sight.

Our route from the ferry to Hotspring Island was now being reversed. After about 13 miles of paddling, Krista and I arrived at the arranged campsite, and met up with the comical brothers. They fried us a slab of steak for supper and we all enjoyed another hilarious evening.

Day 61 13th June

We commenced the day in style, with a breakfast of bacon and eggs and afterwards, canoed northwards leaving the brothers struggling with their packing. We intended to have plenty of breaks for fishing and at our first fishing stop, Kevin and Rob caught up and overtook us.

A headwind blew up in the afternoon and we were again paddling as a foursome. The extra effort needed against the wind gave them backache and a few problems with steering. Our backs had ached for the first month of the trip, but now we had no trouble.

Kevin's map was more detailed than ours and on it was marked the village of Tanu, a deserted Haida Indian village. The Haida were the local tribe inhabiting the Queen Charlottes, and their influence is still strongly evident in much of coastal British Columbia. They were an ancient tribe, renowned for their outstanding art work and advanced culture. They were also ferocious warriors who travelled long distances by sea, and were famed for their fierce resistance to early Russian attempts at colonisation. Early this century, a smallpox epidemic swept through several Haida villages and, in some cases, wiped out the entire population. In some villages the dead could not be buried quickly enough and the bodies were buried in open graves.

At Tanu we parked the boats on the beach and wandered into the forest. The Haidas lived in wooden, communal dwellings known as long houses and each family had a totem pole erected outside their house as a monument to their heritage. The remains of the long houses were outlined by several robust, wooden supports that stood in a line about twenty yards apart. Each support had rectangular holes carved through them, in which a solid, heavy plank rested. Each plank was about two feet across and six inches wide, and were ingeniously hand carved from a large tree. Other 'planks' lay on the ground, covered with moss, but were conspicuous by their regular, angled corners. Room-sized pits lay in a line, alongside the supports, indicated the living areas. It was easy to imagine the once thriving fishing community that lived in the long house at Tanu. The village was now dead and the silent forest was slowly engulfing it. The totem poles had already vanished, except for one half-carved log that lay over two fallen trees above the encroaching sphagnum moss.

We walked through the village in silence and at the end came across the broken headstone of a tomb. Inscribed on it were the simple words, 'In memory of Charlie', and a nearby square pit indicated a past exhumation. Once out of the cold shadows of the forest, the sun warmed us and we continued on our journey.

That evening Rob taught us that art of making bread on a stick. The Canadians call it 'Bannock Bread', but it was soon christened 'Buttock Bread' because it was white, warm and good to get your teeth into! The dough was made by mixing flour, oil, salt, sugar, baking powder and water to a good consistency. A lump of the dough was then attached to the end of a thick stick and held over the embers until it turned brown. The result was delicious bread, tasting like a smoked scone.

Day 62 14th June

From the moment we left the shore it was a struggle, more so for Kevin and Rob than for us because their kayaks rode high above the water, acting like sails in the cross wind.

After a long hard day, Krista and I arrived in Skedans Bay well before our companions and got a welcoming fire going. An apparently un-occupied fishing vessel was moored in the bay and, close to that, the grey whale was still swimming in exactly the same place as it was the last time we visited.

We erected the tent and waited for the brothers to arrive. Setting up camp was now second nature to us and, on a dry day, it only took about half an hour to carry the boats, pitch the tent, light a fire and start cooking. At the beginning of the trip it took us about three hours!

Early in the evening, as we sat around the fire cooking 'buttock' bread and telling jokes, a strange, shrieking sound came from the nearby trees. It sounded like an excited crow, so we shouted at it to shut up. The screeches continued for several minutes, so Kris and I went to investigate. We found a tiny fawn bleating in agony and fear. At first we thought it was caught in a trap, but as we got nearer I saw the culprit. A ginger, stoat-like creature had the fawn's hind leg clamped between its jaws and was twisting and writhing agressively, in an attempt to break it. If the leg had broken the fawn would be as good as dead. Our movements towards the two animals forced the marten to release its grip. This gave the fawn a chance to get shakily to its feet and stagger to its helpless mother. The marten hissed its hatred at us and went in pursuit of its escaped prey via a series of burrows and tree roots. The doe, safely re-united with her young, caught sight of the marten and, in gallant protection of her family, chased it to a recess, amongst some pine roots, and lashed out viciously with her front hooves. It was a display of aggression rarely seen in this normally gentle species, and the marten was lucky to escape unhurt.

We returned to the fire, understanding that this natural battle would continue until the fawn reached sufficient size and maturity to fend for itself. The marten, although temporarily beaten, would persist in attacking the fawn until it was either successful or another easier subject came along.

Two of the occupants of the moored fishing boat ambled past us with a line full of trout. They were from Vancouver and the skipper of the vessel, had given the crew a rest day. The boat was called the 'Arctic Ocean' and, judging by the large suspended drum, was a seine fishing vessel. They tow a large bell-shaped net which is winched aboard by a heavy duty seine winch to unload the catch. On this trip, however, the crew were not fishing commercially. Instead they had three marine biologists aboard who were taking samples for research and, to the disgust of the fishermen, they had to throw everything they caught back into the sea.

The two fishermen joined us in drinking several tots of whisky and then invited us on board for some fish. They stipulated that women were not allowed on the boat, so I drew straws with Kevin and Rob to see who would go aboard. I picked the lucky short straw and, an hour before darkness fell, I paddled out to the boat, making a detour to visit our friendly whale first.

The crew were a rough-and-ready bunch, dressed in unwashed jeans, and check shirts. They welcomed me on board like a brother and showed me around. The bridge, high above the water, was full of instruments and charts; the good fishing areas and danger spots ringed in red ink. The living quarters were comfortable but most of the space below deck was taken up by a refrigerated fish hold. We drank coffee and swapped jokes and stories, while the three, timid-looking biologists sat and politely smiled at the punch lines.

The skipper was reading a book about how the Germans castrated Jews during the war and every now and then he shared his interest in the subject by reading a passage or two to the crew.

'How did you cross Queen Charlotte's Sound?', the cook asked. 'We just followed the coast round Cape Caution' I replied.

'Wow, you've got more balls than the whole crew put together!' 'Yes', I said, 'and one of us is a woman!' He laughed and ploughed back into his dirty mag. They all had a three word vocabulary, MF, CS, and P. and although it was obviously painful to the biologists, they were too polite to say anything. The boat was to sail at dusk across Hecate Strait and ultimately to Vancouver, where the biologists planned to collate their information and the fishermen to organize their next trip.

Before I left the 'Arctic Ocean' the cook heaved a 175lbs halibut on to the working deck, and cut some steaks from the tail with a razor-sharp knife. He was an expert at his trade, gauging the width of each individual vertebrae to perfection. Pacific halibut are capable of growing to a weight of up to 700lbs. The 175 pounder I was looking at was about 6 feet in length. They are a 'bottom' fish which are reputedly easy to catch, but which have so far eluded us.

The main feature of the Pacific halibut is its strength. When fishermen catch a large halibut nowadays, they shoot it in the head before hauling it aboard. Fishermen who fail to kill the halibut before landing it have been known to be maimed or even killed by a flapping fish in the holds of their own boat.

The crew of the 'Arctic Ocean' helped me back into the kayak and their final advice was, 'Let go of your line if you get a big 'un.'

Back on shore we fried some of the steaks and watched the lights of the 'Arctic Ocean' cruise out of sight. I can now understand why halibut meat is regarded to be as much of a delicacy as salmon.

Day 63   15th June

The tide was a long way out in the morning so, to avoid carrying the boats, we decided to walk along the beach to try and find Skedans Indian village, which had proved to be so elusive on our way south.

After a couple of miles our journey was halted by a precipitous bluff and we were forced to return to the kayaks. Krista and I paddled in

Skedans Village, a Haida Indian totem pole

A silly place to camp (at the end of a runway)

Kevin's and Rob's boats, past the resident whale, to a small sandy beach, just beyond the bluff that had impeded our progress earlier.

A short way into the trees we found an erect totem pole, which had been expertly carved by the Haidas early this century. After a further search we discovered another seven totem poles. Some were lying flat on the ground, completely covered with moss, while others were leaning at various angles. Only two of the poles remained upright. The wood was weathered, grey and badly decayed but the distinctive eagle and beaver family emblems could be seen. In this rain forest, once the poles fall and come in conact with the ground, they become engulfed by moss within months. If they remain upright, decomposition is slower. We were looking at some of the few original artefacts of Haida heritage, realising there would probably be little trace of them in 30 years.

The Haidas were an exceedingly creative tribe. With an abundance of natural food in the forests and the sea, they had ample time to devote to creative activities. Another curious fact was that they were almost Caucasian in appearance and thus easily distinguishable from other Native tribes. Like Tanu, the population at Skedans was decimated by smallpox at the turn of the century. It was more expedient to bury the dead in open graves and, to this day, a grisly pile of moss-covered skulls still remains in the woods of Skedans village.

Later in the day we parted company with Rob and Kevin. This was their last canoeing day and, as they left, we arranged to meet them in Sandspit Airport bar before they flew back home.

As they disappeared into the distance behind us, the water ahead swarmed with bald eagles. A flock of about fifty of the birds soared and swooped in excitement over a small patch of sea. It was a magnificent sight but we failed to discover the reason for their frenzy. The tide was with us and, despite the beds of floating kelp, we made good progress. At one stage a seaplane flew straight between us, almost skimming the sea. It was so close that we could see the smiling face of the pilot and his waving passenger.

Shortly before setting up camp I was startled by a splash behind me and had a fleeting view of a torpedo-shaped object darting beneath my boat. I soon realised that it was only a friendly sea lion following us for company.

Day 64 16th June

The day started badly with the longest and most tiring boat-carry to date. From striking camp to launching took us over two and a half hours of strenuous work. The beach sloped gently and the tide was very low. It would have been easy if the beach had been sand, but this one was made up of round, unstable boulders covered in thick seaweed, which made traction an impossible dream.

By the end of the struggle we were both irritable and fed up but, once on the water, a strong current took us to Sandspit. The surrounding land was low and flat and we managed to avoid being drenched by black clouds that swept across the sea, discharging their damp cargoes in front and behind us.

As its name suggests, Sandspit is built on a sandspit and it consists of a small airport and a few roads lined with neatly kept houses. We had failed to visit Sandspit on the way south because we had been distracted by a whale, so we made up for it now by exploring the village. On returning to our camp we were shocked to find that we had pitched our tent about twenty feet from the end of the airport runway. We hadn't realised our mistake earlier because a pile of driftwood had obscured the view. Despite its obvious drawbacks we decided to stay put, and lit the fire where the smoke would not distract the pilots.

Earlier in the week, Krista had found a glass fishing float amongst the debris on the beach. The glass was pale blue in colour and shaped like a hollow rolling pin. Two people we met in the evening, who joined us for pancakes, told us that the 'Charlottes' were the best islands in Canada for finding fishing floats. Most of the floats are spherical in shape and drift over from Japan on the Japanese current. They told us that the float Krista had found was relatively rare and had originated in Korea.

Day 65   17th June

We were woken early by the thunderous noise of an aircraft flying low overhead. We tried to have a lie in but, considering the noise, we did well to stay in bed until about 10am. The tent looked ridiculously small and out of place, under the shadows of the aeroplanes that flew above but nevertheless between flights, our morning was relaxed and we concentrated on building up our energy reserves. In the afternoon we paddled to a beach on the other side of the town. The evening brought a pleasant sunset over the islands and we sat, well into the early hours, sipping beer and watching the moon shimmering on the sea.

Day 66 18th June

The early morning sun was bright and unusually warm and the day seemed even more beautiful as we tucked into a breakfast of bangers and chips.

At 11am we met Robin and Kevin in the bar for our final 'good-byes'. After an hilarious session of exaggerated stories about their adventures they flew on the 1pm plane. Once they had left, things started to get a little hazy mainly due to the fact that we had achieved the impossible, and become drunk on American beer! We met a total stranger named Cec White, who took us back to his home for a meal with wine, liqueur ice cream and yet more beer. He was determined that we would not leave the Charlottes sober. At 9pm, and several liqueur ice creams later, he helped us load the boats on to his truck, and then drove us five miles down the road to a position opposite the ferry terminal. Somehow, we managed to paddle the two miles to the ferry and once we were safely aboard, we met a chap from the local hatchery, who knew Kevin. He poured us some whisky and insisted that we drank it. Krista met a nasty, lecherous little man who took a fancy to her and just would not leave her alone. He persisted in telling her that he liked the hardy types and he wished he could do a trip with her. We both got annoyed with him and, in a vague attempt to creep back into our favour, he said, 'You two must be something special to do a trip like this.' I replied truthfully, 'No, any moron can do it if they put their minds to it.' He looked visibly shocked thinking that I had called Krista a moron.

The crossing was calm but even so we both slept badly. Krista was battened tightly into her sleeping bag as an 'anti-nasty little man' tactic, but the main reason for our lack of sleep was a crowd of noisy kids who found that our weary bodies on the deck made an excellent obstacle course to run around.

Chapter Four: **Sights on Alaska**

Day 67 19th June

At 5am a siren blasted and this was our cue to crawl out of our pits and stagger to the standing position. Out of the window, in the half light of dawn, we recognised the familiar structures lining the approaches to Prince Rupert. Krista had a diabolical hang-over and we paddled, in the morning mist, along the Prince Rupert shoreline in a complete daze. We passed Chinese, Japanese and Russian ships in the harbour and continued past the dormant fishing fleet, to the jetty we had used on our previous visit.

Today was a day of business. We wrote letters, bought charts, shopped for food and collected supplies that we had sent from Vancouver. The kayaks were moored over a mile from the Post Office, so we borrowed a trolley from a supermarket to transport the heavy boxes to the boats. En route, our trolley developed acute steerage problems and, under the weight of our supplies, collapsed twice on the way to the dock. We soon discovered that trolleys were not designed to traverse level crossings, and we had not previously noticed that the docks had a network of railway lines!

Packing the boats was a major task that brought back memories of our first 'pack' in Vancouver. The food had to be divided into packs of equal volume and, as we did this, many passers-by stopped to chat with us. Most refused to believe that the packages would fit in the boats, but by late afternoon we had completed the task satisfactorily.

A quick 'burger' sustained us for the paddle out of Prince Rupert and by 4.30pm we set off across the Sound. We canoed past a Japanese ship, to the unpopulated shore opposite Prince Rupert. The tide was high so we did not have to carry the boats far and by 7pm we were fast asleep!

Day 68 20th June

The boats felt extremely heavy with all the extra food and this, combined with a stiff breeze and an inconsistent tide, resulted in us only managing ten miles. In the distance we got our first glimpse of Alaska in the form of pale, grey mountains on the far horizon.

Wildlife seen today consisted mainly of seals, many with small, fluffy pups. Seals were normally very timid in the wild but these basked on

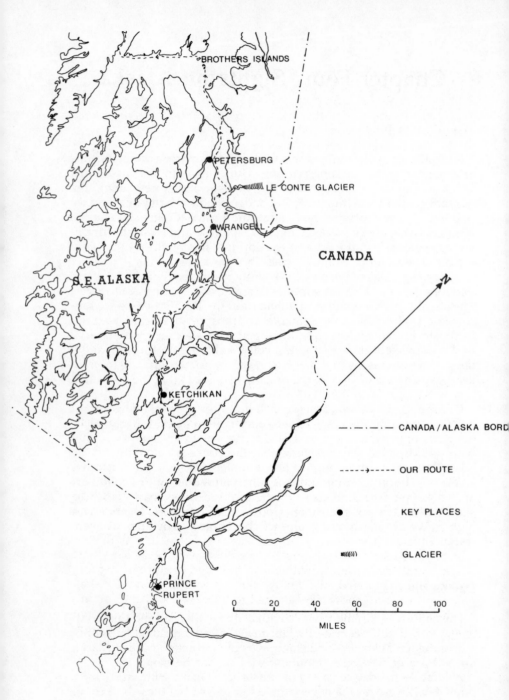

The route from Prince Rupert to Petersburg

the rocks and allowed us to draw very close to them. We had noticed that many seals, when in shallow water, lie on their bellies with their tails and heads above the surface, in a banana shape. The inquisitive 'bananas' amused us but there is a practical reason for adopting this pose. The tail area, in relation to the well-insulated body, is very rich in blood because the capillaries are most concentrated there. The tail can thus be used in one of two ways. Firstly as a means of losing heat (similar to the way elephants flap their ears to cool down), the capillaries dilate and come nearer to the surface to allow heat loss. Secondly, as a means of gaining heat, the tail can be raised above the water to receive sunlight and to increase the body temperature through the circulating blood. The difference between the two functions is that the tail is kept wet for heat loss, and dry for heat gain.

Our camp was on a sandy beach on Swamp Island. Firewood was plentiful and the food excellent but poor Kris was still 'hung over' from Monday. We had purchased some vitamin tablets in Prince Rupert to supplement our diet, so we are trying to monitor our moods and spirits to see if they work.

Day 69   21st June

Today was warm for the whole day. It was, after all, Mid-Summer's Day and also Krista's birthday. We took advantage of the pleasant weather and paddled steadily northwards, making easy work of the heavy boats. After some fifteen miles we struck an early camp on the sandy beach of a small island north of Port Simpson.

Whilst exploring the island, we discovered a berry that neither of us had seen before. It grew on tangled, brambly bushes and was conspicuous by its bright, pinky red colour. It looked like a blackberry but was twice the size and its brambles were not so prickly. Cautiously, we sampled the berries and found them to have the flavour of a raspberry. Krista's birthday meal turned out to be a real treat; fresh steak, from Prince Rupert, with chips, followed by our newly-found berries and evaporated milk. Before dark we walked round the island and, on the north shore, we stopped to look across Dixon Entrance to the first mountains of Alaska. We had now paddled well over halfway and the next stage of the trip promised to be interesting, and we speculated on what lay ahead with a tingle of excitement.

Dixon Entrance was the next stretch of water we had to cross and, like Cape Caution a few weeks previously, was one of the few places where there was no alternative route if the weather became unfavourable.

Further around the island we disturbed an eagle which, in panic, flew out of the trees in front of us. This was the closest we had been to an adult eagle and we were surprised at its size. The wing span must have exceeded five feet. Suddenly more noise erupted from the trees and some twenty five bald eagles flew from the woods in front of us, in groups of two's and three's. They circled high in the sky, riding the thermals. We observed for a while and then continued with our walk. Only then did the eagles descend and re-group in the trees. Eagles live mainly on carrion and we guessed that there was probably a carcass on the forest floor that they were interested in.

A spectacular sunset descended over the hills in the evening and we both slept soundly, feeling safe in the remoteness of the island.

Day 70 22nd June

In the morning mist it was easy to understand why S.E. Alaska was called 'The land of the Greys'. The sea was like a grey mirror, reflecting the overcast sky and the range of hills that stretched far to the horizon, were of varying shades of grey. On this particular day, our equipment provided the only colours. The glassy water made it easy for us to make positive headway and the whole atmosphere was one of tranquillity.

To cross the thirty miles or so of Dixon Entrance, we chose a route which hugged the coast. Although this was longer than a direct traverse, it narrowed down the exposed crossings and offered us the chance of landing quickly if the weather turned foul.

As we commenced the four mile crossing of Portland Inlet, the weather seemed reasonably stable, but after about a mile we became aware of a slight swell. This increased halfway across and the tell-tale dark patch appeared on the sea warning of wind coming from the west. Soon the swell steepened and broke on the crests, and the calm atmosphere of the morning totally disappeared in the hissing wind. We kept close together and aimed for a small island directly ahead. Time seemed to pass slowly and after a while most of our strokes were directed at balance and steering, rather than forward motion. The wind became colder and the spray chilled our hands but, very slowly, we neared Tracey Island hoping to find refuge from the storm. The dark, low clouds moved speedily above us and the waves crashed violently against the land ahead. It soon became apparent that Tracey Island had vertical cliff sides which, in these conditions, made landing impossible. The mainland beyond the island had similar terrain, with sheer thirty foot rocks guarding the land from the sea. We had no choice but to press on around the coast in the hope finding a break in the cliffs. Bearing westwards into the storm we kept parallel with the coast, at a safe distance from the pounding waves.

Hugging the coast produced a further obstacle to impede progress. The waves rebounded back to sea from the cliffs, thus intensifying the incoming swell. When incoming wave crests meet rebounding waves from the cliffs, their height almost doubles and, if the crests are particularly steep or breaking, when they collide, the resultant explosion of water sprays in what is known as a clapotis. The only way to avoid them was to stay out of the immediate danger area by canoeing about half a mile from the shore.

Around the headland another cluster of islands came into view, so we aimed for them. We reached the first island after an exhausting and nerve-wracking hour of paddling. On the leeside of the island the sea became calmer but the rocks were still too steep for landing. At a distance, all the islands looked the same but on closer inspection, we discovered that one was completely out of character with the others. It was sandy! Our spirits were raised and we began the final two miles to the sand, thankful that the end of our ordeal was close.

We landed shortly before dusk and the warmth and security of our tent was a great comfort after an exceptionally hard and harrowing day.

Day 71 23rd June

Despite the irresistable attraction of a sandy beach, we were once again reminded that camping and sand just do not mix, especially when it's raining. As we struck camp, three killer whales swam close to the shore in about fifteen feet of water, and about half an hour later they re-appeared the other side of the channel. They are extremely strong looking beasts and it surprised us to learn, that these carnivorous whales are capable of flipping themselves, seventy to eighty feet up a beach to catch seals, before returning to sea to finish the meal.

After leaving the island we crossed the Alaskan border, and continued along the exposed western shore following a rugged coastline similar to yesterday. In the morning the weather had calmed but by afternoon the swell increased and we had another rough time in a very confused sea. We passed a fishing boat and the occupants cheered us on with shouts of 'You're crazy', 'You're dead' and other similar witticisms designed to boost our confidence.

Landing was again virtually impossible but, before it got too late, we managed to sneak in through the breakers and weave our way between a few foaming rocks, to a relatively calm cove. At the rear of the cove a strange looking scaffold arched seaward from a rock and, leading from it, we discovered a stilted narrow-gauged railway, that disappeared into the forest. We walked along the bizarre-looking railway and after a mile or so it ended at a tall, white, rectangular lighthouse. Inscribed above the door were the words, 'U.S. Coastguard. 1900. Strictly no trespassing'. The lighthouse had obviously been manned at one stage but was now totally automatic. It looked so cosy that we decided to sleep on the third storey and from our Penthouse suite, we had a good view of the rugged coast stretching away into the mist. To us it looked remarkably similar to parts of Cornwall.

While preparing the evening meal on the stove, Krista attempted a mid-cook refuel but the operation came to an untimely end when the fuel inside the bottle ignited and she dropped it. In minutes our home for the night was in flames and black smoke billowed from the windows. We rescued the sleeping bags and desperately tried to extinguish the fire, because we didn't want to draw attention to ourselves in this way. Luckily there were no witnesses and we were able to move back in when the flames had subsided.

Day 72   24th June

During the night the drizzle and rain blew in through the open windows and our sleeping bags resembled soggy rags in the morning! There was quite a wind blowing so, dejectedly, we walked back along the stilted railway to the boats, and had a 'pig-out' session on pancakes to pass the time. Later, the wind abated sufficiently to make a start, and at about 3pm we pulled out into a steady swell. We were surprised to encounter scores of fishing boats along the way and a shouted conversation with one crew, kicked off with them yelling the inevitable, 'You're crazy'. Apparently the abundance of fishing boats in this area was because most other areas had been closed in preparation for the salmon runs. In order to conserve salmon stocks, various areas are open or closed, on selected dates, by the Department of Fish and Game. To be caught fishing in closed areas means severe fines or confiscation of boats and tackle. Such stiff penalties were enough to ensure the fishermen obeyed the rules.

In the evening, whilst planning the next section of our route, we discovered that we had lost the chart covering the next 100 miles of the journey. 'Oh, well', quipped Krista, 'worse things happen at sea!' We had now canoed 755 miles since leaving Vancouver.

Day 73 25th June

The worst of the storm died out overnight and progress became easier. Again there were many fishing boats in the area, laying nets and vying for the best spots near stream and river mouths. The salmon had just started their annual spawning runs and, quite regularly, they leapt clear of the water nearby. Salmon converge on Canadian and Alaskan streams from all over the North Pacific, and each individual salmon returns to spawn and die in exactly the same stream where it was hatched. This annual migration attracts commercial and sports fishermen from all over North America, and if the fish are lucky enough to avoid being caught by humans, there are always the bears to contend with. Bears descend on the streams for their summer protein and comparatively easy feeding.

Despite the many obstacles on the way, hoards of salmon still make it to the spawning grounds where, after mating; they eventually die. Eagles then take on a major task of removing the carrion and thus the risk of disease in the rivers is minimised. This feast for the eagles marks the end of the fascinating life cycle of the salmon.

Late in the morning we spotted a bear, and witnessed the almost perfect camouflage of the black bear in a forest environment. We paddled closer for a better view, and found that the bear was nursing a tiny cub. We had a clear view of it and it leaped about like a newly-born lamb. It looked both frail and kitten-like, resembling its mother only in colour. However, we soon saw that it was a natural climber as it scurried up and down trees as easily as a squirrel. Several minutes elapsed before the mother became aware of danger, and she quickly ushered her cub away, with a few grunts, to the safety of the forest. Bears are normally thought to be dumb animals but in times of danger they can hiss, grunt and puff. After a few minutes paddle along the shore, another larger bear was seen loping along the beach. They were certainly becoming more plentiful as we headed north!

Each day since leaving Vancouver we had seen seals. They always seemed to find our campsite in the evening and stare with wide eyes, at our curious activities. On this particular evening we counted over 75 seals, playing the staring game, and many of them were young pups. Although very inquisitive, they were also timid and any approach we made towards them usually sent them splashing away in panic.

In the evening, as we sat sheltering from a slight drizzle, Krista spotted some killer whales. They were swimming casually, against the tide, about half a mile away, diving and surfacing at regular intervals. At the same time, we noticed that the seals had disappeared. There were approximately fifteen whales in the pod, including several calves. One adult orca was particularly conspicuous by its sheer size. Its slightly curved, triangular dorsal fin stood at about six feet in height and its exhalatory puff sounded much louder and deeper than the others. In our excitement, we abandoned the shelter and leapt into the kayaks for a closer look. After a few short strokes into the sea, we 'wimped out' deciding that the whales looked too menacing! We opted instead for another vantage point in the shape of a rocky islet. Before we landed, one of the whales broke away from the group to investigate us, and it circled the island a couple of times with its eye above the water. Others in the main pod, then began to leap out of the water, their huge bodies completely clearing the sea. Each landing echoed around the bay with an explosion of spray. We couldn't believe our eyes, seeing them breach in the wild. I had always thought that such leaping was a trick reserved for the 'circus' whales at 'Sea World'. Soon after the breaching began, other whales started to slap their lateral fins on the sea and after a few minutes, all the young whales followed suit, leaping, slapping and peering out of the water. It was only when one of the whales revealed its row of ivory teeth that we realised why they were such efficient predators. Despite the frivolity of the younger whales, the huge adult orca continued on its steady course against the tide and, after about half an hour, they passed out of sight. We were both ecstatic at having witnessed such a wonderful, natural display and we returned to the tent chattering excitedly about the experience.

A sea mist came in quickly in the evening and shortly before retiring to bed, a ghostly sailing boat drifted silently by, into the eerie mist and once again, our movements were being monitored by the ever-present shiny, black eyes of the seals.

Day 74   26th June

During the night the wind blew up and the rain drummed a heavy rhythm on the tent. The surrounding trees started groaning and the waves began pounding the shore. In the pitch darkenss of the tent, our imaginations ran riot. The sea sounded only a few feet away and the trees threatened to shed branches on us.

At daybreak, it was blatantly obvious that canoeing was out of the question, so we did not emerge from the tent until forced out by hunger. The day was spent eating, writing letters and stalking the seal colony for photographs. The seals lay haphazardly on a large, seaweed covered rock and they gave us the impression that they were also storm-bound. Normally, they disappear into the sea if we approach too close but today, they must have realised that they were safe behind a natural barrier of foaming water.

Day 75 27th June

The storm was still raging in the morning, so we repeated the tactics of yesterday and lay-in. The wind seemed to increase in strength during the day and we spent hours watching the waves and spray as they engulfed the rocks in violent white foam. The seals had vacated their perch because the rock was no longer habitable, and we did not see a sea bird all day. One eagle braved the wind but it struggled to stay airborne and lost control of its flight at every gust.

Our island refuge was so small that streams were non-existant. The only sources of water were the small rock pools, but now these were rendered undrinkable by the constant spraying of sea water. To alleviate our immediate water shortage, we collected rain drops in the saucepan and the run-off from the tarpaulin kept us in reasonable supply. Our main problem though, was that all our food needed large quantities of water for cooking properly.

Day 76 28th June

The storm continued unabated but we were forced to leave the island to find water. For safety, we travelled together and in the confused sea, the one mile crossing to the mainland took three quarters of an hour!

Landing on the mainland was easy. We had aimed at a small cove and this acted as a natural harbour against the breaking waves. At the back of the cove we found a navigable stream, the banks of which were covered in grass and the forest on either side was dense and very green.

We had only canoed about 200 yards upstream when we stumbled across the inevitable. A large, black bear grazing on the grassy bank. Its camouflage was so good that we were almost on top of it before we spotted it. Keeping a wary eye on the bear, we quickly filled the water bottles and drifted silently backwards downstream towards the cove, hoping that none of his colleagues would cut off our retreat by going for a drink.

The risk of returning to the island, across the stormy water, seemed well worth the effort, just to be camping well clear of the bears. That evening we discovered that the stream water we had collected was useless. In our haste to fill our bottles we had not tasted it and unfortunately, it was half sea water. However, looking on the bright side, slightly salty water was suitable for cooking, leaving our small supply of fresh water available solely for drinking.

Our diet was still lacking in certain basic nutritional components and strangely enough our bodies reacted to encourage us to eat certain foods. For example, we were lacking in fats and we both developed an urge to drink cooking oil, thus increasing the fat level in our diet. I assume that this desire for cooking oil will subside when our life style and diet resumes normality.

Day 77 29th June

What a relief! The sun was shining and the sea was in a passive mood. Sea birds were again in flight and the seals had returned to their rock. We ate breakfast in the company of two humming-birds and concocted a sugary meal for them in a bottle lid.

Canoeing was again easy and pleasurable and we managed to cover sixteen miles before the wind started to blow, almost as strongly as the past few days. Our proposed camp on yet another island turned out to be too sheer for landing, so we crossed to the mainland and surfed into a small, log-choked beach that nestled conveniently between some black and unaccommodating cliffs. Seaweed hung in the trees from the previous storm and it was difficult to find a suitable campsite amongst the fallen branches.

Day 78 30th June

The day was again very wet and windy and we were both frustrated at our recent lack of progress. A general air of depression hung over us all day and all we could do was sit under the dripping trees watching for hints of a break in the weather. We were only fifteen miles from the town of Ketchikan but it seemed so very distant. Our campsite was

94

not particularly alluring as the forest was too dense to walk through, and the forest floor was covered in Devil's Clubs. Their six feet long stems are covered with prickles, which have remarkable skin penetrating qualities, so we stayed put.

Late in the evening, the wind abated and the rain ceased, so out of sheer frustration we packed quickly and paddled off in a misty drizzle. On the way we passed a couple of deer scrambling on a stony beach, and a pair of storm-ravaged eagles picking at a dead fish. Shortly before dusk, houses began to appear in the mist and we spotted the headlights of a vehicle moving along a road. It was the outskirts of Ketchikan. We grounded at Race Point and soon had the tent erected in the corner of a car park. A lady, strolling with her dog, spoke to us and she invited us to her house for tea. She and her husband were New Yorkers who, for an adventure, had moved to Alaska five years previously. In conversation we asked about the red berries we had eaten on Krista's birthday. She told us that they were known as Salmon berries, so named because they always matured at the time of the salmon runs and they were the colour of spawning salmon. After a cup of tea we returned to the tent and spent most of the evening drying off in front of a raging fire, before retiring to bed.

Day 79 1st July

Today was the official opening of the salmon runs, near Ketchikan, and the channel leading from the town, was very busy with fishing boats, all sailing early to try and secure the best spots to set their nets. On this occasion the area was only open for three days. The fishing grounds were patrolled very effectively by light aircraft and boats from the Government Fish and Game Department. The reason for the stringent checks and limited openings were to prevent over fishing, and thus ensuring the survival of the Pacific salmon.

During the morning, Krista met a young man with big wellies and tall stories. He told us that his 8 year old brother had once hooked a whale and managed to land it on the very beach where we were sitting. 'They breed tough kids in Alaska!' we thought and when we had tired of his stories we walked the six miles into Ketchikan.

It was definitely a town of character with its attractive wooden buildings set on a steep hillside. It was also a town of numerous fishing boats, totem poles, and over 40 miles of tarmac road. Its only links with the outside world were by sea and air and consequently an expensive tourist area had grown around the waterfront docks.

A calm day near the border of Alaska

Camping scene on a small island

From our observations of people in Ketchikan, one baffling question emerged to which we could not find an answer; 'How can American tourists be so conspicuous in their own country?'

Food stores and Immigration offices were closed today so we could not do very much of our own personal business. Instead we re-lived the trauma of realising how scruffy and odious we were, compared with other people, by sitting in a café and being avoided by everyone.

A very drunk logger gave us a lift back to the tent and his main conversation revolved round his craving to touch ladies.

It is very odd how our mileage averages almost exactly 10 miles a day. A week ago we were well above this average and then suddenly, after three and a half days of being stormed in, our average had again dropped to 10 miles a day.

We have covered 795 miles so far.

Day 80 2nd July

We paddled into Ketchikan early and moored at the fishing jetty. An hour was spent shopping and sending letters, before we presented ourselves for interrogation at the Customs and Immigration offices. Officially, new entrants have to register with Immigration within 24 hours of crossing the border. We had already been in Alaska for over a week but the Officer was sympathetic and gave us permission to remain until the end of the year.

The Customs office was our next call and we wished afterwards that we had avoided it. We were confronted by an officious lady who bombarded us with questions about our kayaks. She had a form to complete and come hell or high water she was going to get the correct answers. The conversation went something like this:

'What's the name of your boat?'

'It hasn't got a name, it's a kayak.'

'What, no name? Then where was it registered and what's its number?'

'It's only a kayak, it doesn't need to be registered.'

'Yes, it does. All vessels need to be registered. How many crew have you aboard?'

'I don't think you quite understand. We are paddling small kayaks and there is no crew, only us.'

'I know that. How big is your liquor cabinet?'

'They haven't got liquor cabinets. They are only kayaks'.

'How much water do you hold below deck?'

'We have only got water bottles and we carry them on deck.'

The questioning continued until it dawned on her that the form did not apply to us. Not to be outdone, she went off on another tack and decided to investigate the origin of the boats. This was dangerous ground because it could have resulted in paying an expensive bond that we could not afford, in order to ensure that we take the boats out of Alaska when we leave. By now I realised that her intellectual capacity was limited, so I told her a pack of lies while Krista stood by amazed at the gullibility of the woman. The lady soon became utterly confused and a more astute colleague came to her rescue by saying, 'Are you smuggling drugs?' 'No,' I replied, and our Customs exercise was rounded off with a, 'Good, have a nice journey and get outta here before she starts up again.'

Soon afterwards, we had the boats packed and we paddled northwards, with a good current, to the outskirts of Ketchikan.

Day 81 3rd July

The main aims of the day were to cross the Behm Canal and catch a salmon. Behm Canal was a six miles wide stretch of water with some unpredictable currents, so we departed early to take advantage of the calm, morning water.

Ketchikan boasted a huge fishing supplies store and yesterday, we had splashed out on an assortment of lures recommended for catching salmon. Soon after launching we put them to the test and trailed them behind our boats. Salmon kept up a tantalisng display by leaping out of the sea every now and then, but they never took our bait. Later in the afternoon when we were halfway across Behm Canal, I felt a tug on my line. I quickly wound it in only to find that the line had broken. I tied another lure and within a few minutes it also disappeared. When the same thing happened to Krista we abandoned fishing for the day. Obviously a heavy creature with sharp teeth, was below us in the deep black water and was biting through our 200lb lines. In one day we had lost 80% of our new tackle!

The wind hit us with a hefty blast, halfway across Behm Canal and Krista pulled a stomach muscle in the supreme effort needed to complete the crossing. On the other side a promising beach beckoned and we decided to call it a day to avoid further strain on Krista. A 'creative' evening ensued with Krista fashioning a new spray deck whilst I created a meal of cod in batter.

98

Day 82 4th July

The tide was extra low in the morning and it took us until midday to get on the water. The carry was long but we took it steadily to prevent further strain on Krista's pulled muscle.

The day was bright and clear and a reasonable current helped us northwards. Porpoises surfaced near the kayaks several times during the day and salmon leapt gracefully around us. Krista managed to hook a fair-sized salmon, and as she wound in, it leapt out of the water several times. Suddenly the line went slack and the fish was lost. Despite all the wasted effort, we did make the discovery that balancing a kayak and fighting a salmon at the same time, was quite tricky. Heartened by our near miss, we continued trolling. Most of the salmon seemed to be leaping close to the shore, especially near the mouths of streams and rivers, presumably to acclimatise to the freshwater journey ahead of them. Working on the theory that our chances of a catch would be better nearer the shore, we edged closer. Without warning 'Twang' - the line snagged the bottom and snapped, thus disposing of our final salmon lure.

Our day ended on a beach of black sand, with an exquisite view of the mountainous borders of Clarence Strait to the north. We had both caught the sun and were in good spirits after a pleasant day in the warm sunshine.

Day 83 5th July

We paddled against a strong current for the first ten miles but were kept happy with numerous sightings of porpoises. Lunch was a disastrous popcorn session, or more accurately a charcoal session, but after consuming our U.S. recommended daily allowance of carbon, we pressed on up Clarence Strait in the bright sunshine, before turning eastwards into Ernest Sound. By late afternoon, the weather had deteriorated and we both felt unusually tired. We consulted the chart and decided to aim for an island about six miles away.

When we arrived about an hour later, we discovered that it wasn't an island but a rocky outcrop, which was linked to the mainland by a short isthmus. Camping there looked unsuitable so we back-tracked a few hundred yards to a beach we had spotted earlier. Within seconds of landing, I saw a bear in the trees and we had no choice but to make a quick exit. A mile or so futher into Ernest Sound was another beach but, as we came near to land, Krista shouted, 'Look, another bear!'

Further on still, yet another bear grazed in the long grass. We came to the conclusion that camping in this area was out of the question because even if we did find a 'bear-free' spot we would be too worried to be able to sleep.

We now pinned our hopes on another island about four miles ahead and, lethargically, we set off with a gentle breeze blowing in our faces. As we approached Sunshine Island looked extremely rocky and almost impossible to land. Why do such things always happen when you are extra tired?

On closer inspection, the island appeared to be 'bear-free' because it was about two miles from land and only about 100 yards in diameter. It was too small for a stream and therefore could not sustain a bear for long. We made a quick circumnavigation of the island and were delighted to find an almost perfect landing beach. The tide was high which meant that we didn't have to carry the kayaks and we soon made camp, grateful for the opportunity to be able to sleep without fear from the local 'population.'

Day 84 6th July

A loud crashing noise in the nearby trees woke us during the night but, in the eerie silence that followed, we slowly realised that it was only a fallen branch.

The early morning was damp and grey but once breakfast was over, the mist filtered away and the surrounding hills became visible. Slowly the sun rose over the peaks and by the time we were on the water, it was a glorious day. At one point Krista noticed a porcupine shuffling along in the grass, so we landed to take a photograph. They were obviously very short-sighted creatures, about the size of a stocky cat. It was covered with long spines which bristled when we approached too close and made it appear much bigger than it actually was. Adapted to life in the forest, its claws were surprisingly long and this particular animal, although ungainly and slow, was extremely competent at negotiating obstacles of twisted wood and foliage. We managed to outflank the rodent long enough to take a few photographs but it soon backtracked into the forest and disappeared into the undergrowth.

Lunch was taken next to a stream which reminded us of those found on Dartmoor.

After lunch, whilst canoeing alongside Deer Island, I saw a large, sandy coloured boulder, in the grassy mouth of a river, around which seemed to be three black bears. I pointed it out to Krista and we set off to investigate. After about a mile, the 'boulder' moved slightly and by the size and colour, we guessed that it must be a moose. Still further on we saw clearly that the 'moose' was, in fact, a grizzly bear! The 'sandy boulder' we had seen was its body and the 'black bears' moving around were its darker head and rump. The other 'black bear' was a dark, rusty coloured cub. Edging nearer, its immense size, humped shoulders and facial features became very clear. The water in the bay was too shallow for safety so we edged quietly to the deeper water which resulted from erosion by the river. Watching the two bears was fascinating and because we were very excited at seeing our first grizzly bear, we kept edging forward for a better view. They appeared to be just as short-sighted as black bears but were far more alert.

We drew alongside each other to steady the boats in preparation for a photograph. I passed the telephoto lens to Kris and, keeping a wary eye on the bears, she began to screw the lens into the camera, using the minimum amount of noise and movement. Suddenly and without warning, the bear leapt to the standing position with its arms aloft and its great chest heaving. In the shock of the moment, the telephoto lens flew into the air and plopped out of sight into the sea. Meanwhile, the bear stood on its hind legs, rolling its gigantic head from side to side, hissing, huffing and bellowing with steamy breath drifting from its mouth. The cub imitated the stance of its mother for a few seconds, and then they dropped on to all fours and ran, with an easy lope, into the woods.

We estimated the height of the bear to be about eight feet. We learned later that when bears stand on their hind legs and shake their heads from side to side, it is usually to get a better view of the danger ahead and not a sign of aggression.

When asking Alaskans what the difference is between a brown bear and a grizzly bear, you can expect a variety of answers. Most say the difference is in the size, the grizzly being the larger. Others say that grizzlies live north of Frederick Sound and browns live south. Some say that browns are coastal bears and grizzlies live inland. Sportsmen say that grizzlies are hunted 40 miles inland and the browns nearer the sea. One person told us that grizzlies smell of rotten cabbage and that browns don't smell. A scientist we met told us that there are actual anatomical differences which are very subtle and not obvious to the untrained eye. He got side-tracked and never did enlighten us as to the differences.

Our evening camp was a bit of an anti-climax. It was in a dreary cove which rarely saw the sun. Old scratch marks on the nearby trees indicated that a bear had once claimed the spot as its territory, but we opted to take the risk and stay the night.

Day 85   7th July

A steady but awkward wind plagued us all day and, after about 11 miles, we landed on Zimovia Island in the Zimovia Channel. Fatigue forced us to make an early camp and we ate a good meal of cod and vegetables before bed.

There are many Russian names in S.E. Alaska which date back to the early 1800's when it was a Russian colony. Alaska is still known by some as Seward's Folly' after William Henry Seward, the American Secretary of State, who in 1867 advised his government to purchase the territory from Russia for 2 cents an acre. At the time it was considered to be a foolish buy but this was before oil, coal and gold were discovered. A few groups of people of Russian descent still live in S.E. Alaska, speaking their native Russian tongue and following their traditional way of life.

Day 86   8th July

Taking advantage of a calm day, we continued up Zimovia Channel towards the small town of Wrangell. The narrow channel was dotted with hundreds of coloured marker buoys to each of which was attached a crab pot. The local cannery was limited to a season of two weeks per year for catching crabs so a blitz was under way to reap the maximum harvest.

Camp was set up on a steep, gravel beach 5 miles south of Wrangell. We watched a local man fishing from the beach and he seemed to be doing extremely well. He explained that 90% of the fish he was catching were Bull Heads. They were pesky fish which took the bait readily but were not worth eating due to their small size. Each time he caught a Bull Head he clubbed it and tossed it up the beach to prevent it from biting his line again. His quarry was Sea Trout and luckily for us he had been successful. He stated that he would not miss a couple of these beautiful fish and he kindly gave us one each for supper. He gutted them expertly and told us that they were best cooked in foil. Later, we learned that he worked at the local saw mill and that he hunted bear and moose for both sport and meat. On the strength of our recent experiences we asked about the likelihood of a bear attack. His reply was simple, 'They'll leave you alone, if you leave them alone.' This was a great relief and we came to the conclusion that the nearer you were to bear country the less horrific the tales. Accounts of bears we had heard in the States and England were invariably horror stories based on the theory that blood and guts are bound to impress. Local inhabitants had no need to glorify their encounters with bears in the same way that perhaps a hunting tourist or an adventure holiday-maker might.

Although our friend had put our minds at rest regarding bears, we still thought it prudent to throw all the dead Bull Heads back into the sea, once he had left us, to avoid the possibility of a bear visit.

Day 87 9th July

In the early morning we paddled the five miles into Wrangell and moored the kayaks in the harbour. Rain fell heavily on the wooden walkways and drummed a constant rhythm on the tarpaulins of the colourful fishing boats. The harbour was small and compact and at its centre was an island of ornate totem poles which were replicas of original poles fashioned by a famous local Indian, Chief Shakes.

Wrangell is very small and we were able to walk its entire length in a quarter of an hour. It had a rough-and-ready atmosphere about it, with wooden saloon type buildings, fishermen in oil skins and large bearded characters in heavy check jackets. Historically, Wrangell's claim to fame is that it is the only town in the world which has existed at one time or other under the British, Russian and American flags.

The constant rain did not encourage us to stay in Wrangell for long because there was little scope for camping and we could not afford a room for the night. We decided to explore during the day and continue our journey in the evening. At the north end of the town was the odd sounding Pteroglyph beach. Almost buried in the shingle beach were rocks upon which were carved small, ancient Indian inscriptions. Severe weathering made them difficult to spot but once found, they made fascinating viewing. Most of the designs were spirals or 'eye' shapes and apparently their significance has yet to be deciphered.

At about 5pm we walked along the muddy road back to town and left the harbour half an hour later. Our plan was to cross the three miles of sea to a pleasant looking island. However, once at the sea the wind and tide proved too strong for us to make the island before dark, so we pulled in at Pteroglyph beach feeling damp, cold and very tired. The fire took ages to start and, in the rain, it never burned well enough to afford us much warmth. The sleeping bags were damp and it seemed an impossible dream that they would ever be dry again.

Chapter Five: **Sculptures on Camp Island**

Day 88 10th July

The constant rain and dampness of our surroundings created a distinct air of lethargy and we did not launch until about 12.30pm. The fire had been difficult to start and the boat packing chore took longer than usual. Whenever it rained we could always reckon on at least an hour extra to set up or strike camp and to cook.

A few miles north of Wrangell, the Stikine River reaches the sea and the channels of its delta fan out into mighty branches. The Stikine, we were told, is the fastest navigable river in the world and that it takes several miles of the ocean to check its velocity and absorb its waters. The river is fed by twenty six major glaciers and shortly after leaving Wrangell, the sea temperature took a noticeable plunge.

Our first task for the day was to island-hop across the delta but our intended route was considerably lengthened by the unpredictable currents of the Stikine. The silty river flowed far too strongly for us to ferry glide across its entirety in a straight line but, luckily, the four crossings on our route were all under three miles and necessity gave us the extra strength to negotiate each one. The current was not the only obstacle we encountered in the Stikine Delta. Vast deposits of silt had built up over the years which created an intricate maze of shallows, channels and sand bars. At low tide, the aptly named 'Dry Strait' played havoc with our progress. Frequently the shallows slowed us down and on some sections we had to get out and drag the boats to the next channel. This continued for about two hours until the rising tide came to our aid and we were able to progress by paddle only. Needless to say, larger boats never use this route!

The Stikine Delta is reputed to be an excellent area for spotting moose but the only wildlife we encountered were thousands of midges. The brackish waters of the delta swamp lands made a perfect breeding and hatching place. Once we were in motion they were not too much trouble, but as soon as we stopped to drag the boats through the shallows, swarms of midges and mosquitoes descended upon us and drove us mad with their angry bites. Krista's face and hands swelled up and we vowed to get clear of the Stikine Delta before setting up camp. Our sights were on Coney Island, a thickly-forested, dome shaped island on the far side of the delta. From its location it appeared to be reasonably bear-proof and midge free but unfortunately, the nauseating little creatures followed us all the way and even recruited a few more squadrons en route!

We were both physically drained when we arrived at Coney Island and the thought of camping there was not one we relished. If we stayed the night and the insects continued sucking our blood at the same rate, we would be transparent by morning! So as a last ditch hope for a midge-free night, we set out for Camp Island, some five miles across Frederick Sound.

Ten miles beyond the island stood Le Conte Glacier, and even from our present location 15 miles distant, it appeared huge and majestic. Only the top half was visible between the hills but its source was clear. An ice-cap lay in jagged confusion over the mainland mountains feeding Le Conte Glacier by the constant weight of ice, grinding slowly downward to the sea. Le Conte is the most southerly active tide water glacier in the northern hemisphere and it constantly discharges icebergs into the sea.

Halfway across the Sound, a cold glacial wind blew up. Such winds tend to be localised around glaciers and are caused by the frigid air descending at speed down the huge icy path. Normally, a few miles from a glacier, it is not unusual for the wind to cease quite abruptly. The wind was a blessing in disguise, for although it slowed us down, it certainly got rid of the midges.

Nearer the island we passed lumps of ice coasting along with the tide. Some were a deep blue in colour, while others were white or transparent. Most were the size of a rowing boat and the steely-grey water slapped against them as if to hurry them on. I accidentally bumped into one with my kayak and it did not budge. They were like floating rocks and it was not difficult to understand how they could easily knock a hole in the side of an ocean-going ship.

As we manoevered the kayaks through the floating icebergs towards Camp Island, wolves in the nearby hills heralded nightfall. It was an eerie sound that reminded us that we did not belong in this wilderness and that we were only temporary visitors passsing through.

Once we had landed we were overjoyed to find a wooden cabin with its door open. We entered and found that it was equipped with bunk beds, arm chairs and a wooden table and chairs. There was also a pile of dirty magazines and a pack of cards. Absolute bliss and well worth the effort! Today had been the longest and most strenuous of the trip and the reward of a cabin, after a gruelling 25 miles paddle, worked wonders for our morale.

Day 89 11th July

In the light of day we discovered that the cabin was the property of a 'Hunters' Club' and on the wall a note read, 'Passers-by, make yourselves at home, use anything you find, but please leave the cabin in one piece when you go'. It had obviously not had any visitors for some time and, under both porches, birds had built their nests. In each nest five chicks squeaked uncontrollably whenever an adult arrived with some food. The parents were certainly kept busy flying back and forth between the nests and their food source.

At low tide, the Stikine sandbanks stretched for miles into the distance and blocks of ice, the size of cars, lay stranded on the flats looking oddly out of place on the sand. We walked around the island and on the 'Le Conte' side, the water was heaving with ice. The glacier could be seen ten miles away, looming above the valley sides and stretching beyond into the mountains. All the floating ice we could see had, at some time, been a part of this natural, powerful land carver. The whole scene looked peaceful but the constant noise of grinding and colliding ice contradicted the vision. Occasionally a block would roll over without warning creating a loud thunderous rumble and sharp 'pistol shots' rang out whenever the thawing ice split deep within.

The power and weight of these relatively small pieces of ice had us both fascinated and even small lumps, the size of a child's beach ball, were impossible to lift off the ground. This was the first time that I had seen a tide water glacier and only now could I really begin to understand how glaciers shaped the land, affected climate and transported boulders with their might.

In the afternoon we had a paddle amongst the ice and discovered that the channel was not so congested with ice as it first appeared, and there was ample space to manoeuvre the kayaks safely through. At once stage a 'bungalow-sized' ice lump suddenly overturned close by. It sent up a wave that, with a tremendous crash, threw pieces of ice in every direction. Our lesson was learned the easy way and from now on, we would have to keep clear of the larger ice blocks when we ventured close to a glacier.

Our paddling today was experimental so that we could adapt to the new conditions. We were fascinated to find how the colours of the icebergs differed. Some were navy blue or turquoise whilst others were white or transparent. The densest ice was navy blue with the colour turning from light blue to white or transparent as the ice melts. The hardness of the ice was difficult to conceive and even a mountaineer's ice axe would not scratch it! The glacier ice we were observing had fallen as snow hundreds of thousands of years ago and only now was

106

Grounded Ice lumps on Camp Island

A berg from Le Conte Glacier

being allowed to escape its icy grip.

To round off an excellent day we had a large meal and then discovered a 'fridge half full of very old beer cans. Two or three had ruptured and leaked their contents so, to save the others from a similar fate, we set about drinking them whilst playing cards by candlelight.

Day 90   12th July

For most of the night, the rumbling of falling ice could be heard in the distance and, before breakfast, we took a short walk to see the fascinating lumps of floating ice. We launched the kayaks two hours before high tide, and weaved our way through the ice into Le Conte Bay. The bay was actually a steep-sided channel, uniform in width and seen on the map as a double S shape. It stretched for about 10 miles and led to the snout of the glacier. Because of the shape of the inlet, ice tended to choke on the inside corners and move swiftly on the outside bends. Once we had entered the bay, the ice became thicker and the further in we paddled, the larger the icebergs became. A continuous groan of tortured ice accompanied us as we drew near to the source and at times a loud rumbling sound, identical to a thunder clap, rang out heralding the birth of another iceberg.

Great care had to be taken in the timing of a trip up an inlet such as Le Conte Bay, particularly if the journey was being made in a craft as fragile as ours. When the tide floods the channel fills and brings back all the ice. On the ebb, the ice flows out again. Consequently, if you arrive at the head of the channel before the flood tide begins, the water is comparatively free of ice, but gradually the ice returns with the tide, and can create a potentially dangerous situation.

We planned to allow ourselves two hours to canoe the 10 miles and thus arrive at the glacier at high tide. In this way we would be able to see how much ice was in the channel at maximum flood, and gauge our approach safely. Bearing in mind that floating ice could break or roll without warning we tried to give most of the ice a wide berth, but passing in close proximity was far more intriguing. The cloudy green shapes could be seen lurking below the sea with the clean blue and white tips above the surface. Some of the blocks loomed the height of a two-storey house above us, and it was incredible to think that only about a tenth of the ice was visible above sea level.

Nearer the glacier, the wind grew stronger and because of the peculiar shape of the bay, the glacier only became visible after negotiating the last bend. Thick ice halted our progress some two miles short of the glacier but, in the crisp clear air, it seemed to be much closer. The snout was over a mile across and the whole glacier looked like a giant tongue of bristling blue and white pillars, ready to be pushed by the mass behind them, to their doom in the icy sea. We clung to the precipitous rock slopes of the channel and looked in awe at the sight. A sea of shimmering ice swaying on the swell, was between us and the crumbling glacier face. After a few minutes, we were forced to leave our vantage point as a massive block of ice bumped and scraped its passage along the cliffs towards us. Even with careful timing, some ice had followed us in on the tide and constant steering and manoeuvring was necessary to effect our return journey. The wind suddenly ceased as we retreated back along the passage, but the ice kept us very much on the alert.

Back to the safety of our camp, we soon had a roaring fire going and supper was eaten to the accompaniment of the baby birds chirping. It had been a brilliant day for us and we ended it with some beer next to the fire. By nightfall we were both extremely tired and felt that three months of continuous camping and physical exercise was definitely taking its toll.

Day 91 13th July

Early in the morning we went for a stroll to see the stranded icebergs on the tidal flats. They came in all sorts of bizarre shapes, as if a giant abstract sculptor had fashioned each one individually, and then sprinkled them at random in Le Conte Bay. On a cloudy day such as today, the bluish colours were accentuated beautifully.

On our way back to the cabin we saw wolf tracks in the wet sand. Although the owners could not be seen, the tracks reminded us of newspaper headlines that had monopolised the news just before we began our trip. There had been an international outcry over the mass culling of wolves in Canada and we wondered whether the culling was still in progress.

After a breakfast of pancakes and freshly picked blue berries, we paddled across Frederick Sound, on the first leg of the 17 miles journey to Petersburg.

At midday the silence of the day was taken over by a faint, far away noise which sounded like an approaching train. Slowly, it became louder and louder but its source still had us baffled. Then, we saw it and before we had a chance to don our waterproofs, a torrential blanket of rain swept over us and remained with us for the rest of the day.

At Petersburg the first suitable campsite we found was next to the road near a private house. The house was built on a dump of garden refuse, tin cans and car engines but, to stay sweet with the owners, we thought it advisable to seek permission to camp there. Krista was assigned the task because she had better eye lashes to flutter than me. On this occasion they didn't work and the brusque reply from our temporary neightbours was, 'Yeah, I suppose so, but don't leave any litter!'

Day 92 14th July

It was still raining in the morning and the fire took an eternity to light. The boat carry was lengthy and on slippery rocks, so by the time we had lowered our damp bodies into the cockpits, we were both cold and a little fed up. We paddled to the fishing harbour at Petersburg where we moored the kayaks and headed for town.

Petersburg has a strong Nordic influence and many of its people still speak Norwegian. The main industries, in common with most S.E. Alaskan towns, are fishing and lumbering but Petersburg, although small and rural in appearance has more millionaires per head of population than any other American town. On the surface, however, you would find this difficult to believe. We were told that in Alaska you can tell the people who have 'made it'. They wander around in lumber jackets, jeans and boots. Those dressed in suits are recent arrivals and are trying to 'make it'. There were no suits to be seen in Petersburg during our stay.

Our supplies had arrived safely at the Post Office, so we spent a fair while packing the kayaks. In the nearby harbour a film crew had arrived and were shooting a film about a group of children on their way to the Yukon River. They were a friendly bunch who, in return for shooting some film of us packing the boats, gave us some beer. A large group of people gathered and watched the filming as if we were well known film stars. The camera crew were surprised at our supply of rusty food tins and they zoomed in for close-ups of what they regarded as outrageous health hazards. Before we left, a supply boat laden with fruit, gave us some fresh cherries and the film crew followed us out of Petersburg for a few miles, taking shots and rolling film from different angles. Before bidding them 'farewell' we grabbed some kelp to stop us drifting and joined them in another 'Guinness'. They told us that the kayak shots would liven up the boring children's film, and one jokingly suggested that they should abandon the kids and follow us the rest of the way to Glacier Bay.

Camp was on Kupreanof Island, just across from Petersburg. The kayak carry was hard with the extra weight, but the view of the lights across the water made it a pleasant place to stay.

Chapter Six: **Night Paddle Incentive**

Day 93 15th July

We were surprised to wake to a clear, bright morning, with views of mainland mountains that had previously been obscured by clouds. Unfortunately, we were too tired to fully appreciate our surroundings and concentrated on the hateful task of dragging the freshly laden boats, over logs, to the water's edge.

The weather was kind to us all day and we made an easy 12 mile paddle diagonally across Frederick Sound, to a pleasant beach. Pitching the tent was a problem because the vegetation above the high tide mark grew in an unusually confused tangle, and our first priority was to clear an area in the wet undergrowth. We ate supper next to the fire with a flock of birds and some seals providing the entertainment. The birds were small and flew in tight groups of about 300 in perfect formation. It was mass synchronised flying at its best. At each turn a different part of their bodies became visible and the colour of the whole flock changed at once. It was as if one body was moving and changing shape and colour rather than 300 individuals. Whether they followed a leader or acted on a pre-arranged signal, we could not tell. They certainly kept us amused and virtually hypnotised for about an hour as we watched their performance.

Day 94 16th July

We woke to a wet and windy day so we decided to have a rest. The chop on the sea was indicated by a bell buoy that was out of sight but kept up a constant and enthusiastic peal in the wind.

A huge log fire kept us warm all day and as usual on rest days, we managed to consume abnormal amounts of food. I temporarily lost my appetite after an accident whilst collecting firewood. A very supple stick snapped and the whiplash caught me fair and square in a couple of tender parts. It amused Krista!

Just after this incident we discovered some bear prints in the wet sand. They were obviously fresh as they had not been obliterated by the rain. The alarm bells did not ring too loudly because the prints were those of a small black bear who was obviously eager to avoid an encounter. The tracks did a 180 degrees turn about 30 yards from our camp.

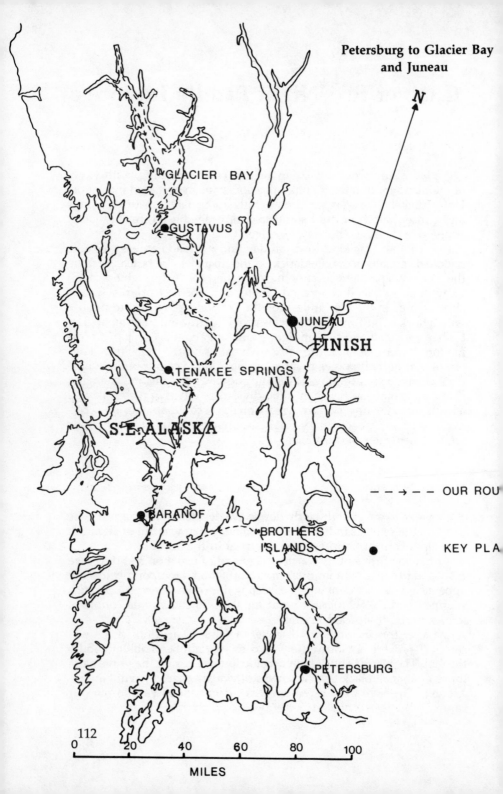

Petersburg to Glacier Bay
and Juneau

N

GLACIER BAY

GUSTAVUS

JUNEAU

FINISH

TENAKEE SPRINGS

S.E. ALASKA

– – –→– – – OUR ROU

BARANOF

BROTHERS
ISLANDS

● KEY PLA

PETERSBURG

112
0   20   40   60   80   100

MILES

Day 95   17th July

We forced ourselves out of the tent at 4.30am to catch the tide and avoid a very long carry. Our campsite had been close to Thomas Bay which, we discovered later, was reputed to be haunted by a tribe of mutant Indians who ended their mortal lives under a giant rockfall. The rockfall, so the story goes, exposed a seam of gold and prospectors visiting the area were either frightened away by the vision of ghosts swarming across the hills towards them, or they died mysteriously shortly after their visit.

At the mouth of Thomas Bay an unusual tide race created some turbulent standing waves and small whirlpools, so we stayed close to each other in case one of us went for an unplanned swim.

On the far side of Thomas Bay we spotted an adolescent black bear ambling along the beach. It was a sleepy-looking animal and was completely unaware of our presence. We canoed alongside it for about three miles and every now and then it stopped and overturned a rock with its paw. Luck was with it on two occasions when it retrieved a dead fish from underneath. The bear loped happily along the beach, climbing over fallen trees in its path, slipping on seaweed and overturning the occasional boulder. It was fascinating viewing and we could have followed it for hours, but the beach ran out and, to avoid the rock face ahead, the bear ambled into the forest and disappeared from sight.

Later in the morning we became extremely cold, so we stopped at the first available beach and prepared breakfast. As we ate, two humming-birds attracted by the bright colours of our clothing, came and hovered within a yard of us. Their small bodies seemed to be suspended in one position as their wings vibrated invisibly and made a sound like a large bumble bee.

By our reckoning we have canoed 999 miles so far!

Day 96   18th July

The sun came out between frequent showers and we managed to cover 20 miles to an island just north of Cape Franshaw. Tomorrow we plan to cross the 12 miles of water to Admiralty Island, so we are hoping for a good day. Shortly before landing for the night, we were looking out to sea at some very large whale spumes, when suddenly there was a deep, powerful sounding puff behind us. We turned quickly and saw the arching back and raised tail fluke of an enormous whale. It was by far the largest we had seen and it was undoubtedly an adult humpback whale. A large humpback grows to about 45 feet in length and can weigh in excess of 50 tons, (the equivalent weight of eight African elephants!)

From our campsite we saw many more and at dusk, before our disbelieving eyes, several leapt clear of the water. We had been impressed when the killer whales had breached a few weeks ago, but to see the massive body of a humpback leap clear of the sea had us cheering with excitement. The strength they must have to generate enough momentum to leap clear of the water is phenomenal. Some of the larger whales could only manage half a breach, but every time they landed, the resulting splash rose slowly into the air in a silent white eruption with the crashing sound reaching our ears several seconds later. Other whales at this time floated on their sides and slapped their huge lateral fins sharply on the sea's surface. This made a splashing sound resembling that of a belly flop from a high diving board! By counting the number of seconds between the leap and the sound of the landing explosion, we calculated that the whales' activity could be heard over three miles away.

Darkness eventually prevented us from seeing the whales but the sound of pounding fins continued well into the night. We could hardly wait to get up in the morning to see them again.

Day 97 19th July

The sound of pounding whale fins woke us before it was light and we lay in the comfort of our sleeping bags, listening to their deep, hollow-sounding exhalations.

It was a calm, sunny day so soon after breakfast we commenced the 12 miles crossing of Frederick Sound. To break the journey we opted to veer slightly northwards to a group of small islands called the Five Fingers. Beyond the Five Fingers lay Admiralty Island, one of the largest islands in the S.E. Alaskan archipelago and which boasts the densest population of brown bears in the world. Fifty miles to the east lay Baranof Island which we could see clearly from our campsite. The spine of the mountains that stretched along its length, soared high above the snow line and in a few days we would be paddling along Baranof's eastern shore and up the long final channel to Glacier Bay.

On the largest of the Five Finger Islands, some five miles into the crossing, stood a lighthouse which was similar in design and size to the one that Krista had almost burnt down a few weeks ago. Calm water enabled us to land at the base of a fixed ladder that ascended vertically for about 50 feet up a concrete rampart. The lighthouse was the last of the manned lighthouses in Alaska and it was in the process of being automated. The lighthouse keepers lived on the rock for 12 month stints and their main recreation was salmon fishing. They were all very friendly and they took us to see their salmon supply. A small wooden shed was stacked to about six feet in height with salmon fillets that they had smoked themselves. We chatted for about an hour and then they presented us with a couple of large fillets from the top of the pile. By then it was time for us to bid them farewell, before our boats became stranded by the ladder on the falling tide.

For the remaining seven miles of the crossing, whales seemed to surround us and the vapour from their breath hung over the water in all directions.

To avoid a camp on Admiralty Island, we chose a campsite amongst a cluster of islands known as The Brothers. A charter boat was moored in a small bay between the two largest islands and we chatted briefly to the crew. About half a mile away a 'Zodiac' inflatable raced back and forth between two whales. The 'Zodiac' carried a group of marine biologists who were busy taking photographs of the undersides of the whales' tails. Apparently the underside of each whale is different, in the same way that fingerprints are different, and this enables scientists to identify individual whales. The humpback is black in colour but under the tail the colouring varies from totally black to totally white with varying shades in between. The white patches are usually symmetrical and the identification of individual whales enables the researcher to ascertain the migration routes and destinations of various whales.

We paddled towards the biologists but kept a reasonable distance from their boat so as not to interfere. We watched as the occupants of the 'Zodiac' manoeuvered behind the whales and trained their lenses on the raised tails. A whoop of joy and applause filled the air each time they were successful. At one stage the whales disappeared for a few minutes then, suddenly, the sea between our boats and the 'Zodiac' began to 'boil' and from the midst of this boiling patch, the wide open jaws of a whale appeared. The jaws surged upwards in a burst of spray and started champing at the air before sinking below the surface again. We had seen a grey whale do a similar thing in the Charlottes but the tremendous size difference made this a much more specacular sight. To us, the jaw movement above the sea looked like a warning signal or a show of power, but the scientists explained that they were only feeding. They feed by diving deeply below the surface and then rising slowly, in a spiral. As they exhale, they create a tubular ring of small bubbles upon which crill, plankton and other small organisms float to the surface. As the 'bubble net' rises, the sea life it contains becomes concentrated at the surface. The whale then swims up underneath the bubbles, with its jaws wide open, and snatches a mouthful of food. Sea birds also know that a 'boiling sea' means concentrated food and they swoop down on a 'bubble net' and make the most of an easy feed. Occasionally, birds get caught in the jaws of a feeding whale and end their lives as whale droppings. Biologists speculate that whales are able to unhinge their jaws for the purpose of 'bubble net' feeding.

Research has shown that there are three distinct migratory whale populations in Alaskan waters and that the same routes are used each year by the same group. Whales in S.E. Alaska migrate for the winter to Baja, Mexico, whilst those in the Bering Sea travel to Hawaii. Whales living in the Aleutians migrate to Japan. Calving in warmer waters is the reason for these migrations but, within a few months, they head north again to the rich feeding grounds of Alaska for their summer feed. It should be added that not all Alaskan whales migrate. There is a small group near Juneau that are known to remain in their home waters.

As soon as a calf is born, the mother whale manoeuvres herself under her offspring and gently pushes it to the surface for its first breath. Once this takes place the calf takes up the normal swimming actions naturally.

We asked the biologists why whales breach and slap their fins. They were not absolutely sure but suggested that it could be mating play, a means of communication or a way of removing barnacles from their skins. During the mating season much of the boisterousness is due to aggressive behaviour between competing males.

Later in the day, we were attracted to an island by the sound of sea-lions. We heard them from about 1½ miles away and we landed and watched some huge males basking on a rock. They were massive animals which emitted sounds like deep, obscene belches. Exploration of the island revealed a much larger colony of about 300 sea-lions, all crammed on a beach some 50 yards long. The combined noise they made was deafening. Nearby I found the jaw bone of a sea-lion with it canine tooth still intact and we were surprised at its size.

Whilst on the island we met Doug, a naturalist from the charter boat, and he invited us to supper. The meal on the 'Observer' was a delight; fresh meat, salad, a variety of desserts and ice cold beer. The biologists spoke mainly about whales and when it was time to leave they insisted on giving us chocolate bars, biscuits, torch batteries, maps, playing cards and herring for salmon and halibut bait. Christmas in July!! It had been an excellent day, rounded off with an enjoyable evening of good food and interesting company. They were moving on the next day but expected to meet up with us in a few days, as they were travelling in roughly the same direction, but taking a 70 mile detour southwards first.

We paddled back to 'Sea-lion' island in the dark and camped on the beach between the two sea-lion colonies. We slept blissfully, with no bear paranoia, despite the incessant belches of our neighbours.

Day 98   20th July

Much of the day was spent observing sea-lions. Their coarse brown bodies seemed totally relaxed as they lay crammed together on the beach with no visible space between them. A strong odour of fat and fish pervaded the air as they sunned themselves and played in the shallows.

Mating season was drawing near and many of the males had open lacerations, inflicted by other competing males. The battles at this time of the year were relatively playful but, as the season gets into full swing and competition becomes more fierce, the fights increase in tenacity and viciousness. The general rule is that the bigger and stronger the male, the larger his territory and harem of females becomes. They collect as many females as they can control and frequently have to ward off other potential suitors. In the meantime, adolescent males practice their future dominating role on the pups by herding them away in small groups from the harems. It has been known for divers, mistaken for female sea-lions, to be herded towards the beach by aggressive and, no doubt, amorous males.

From our observations, it was obvious that they were very short-sighted out of water. They couldn't detect slow movement if you walked directly towards them, but lateral movement was usually detected. Any irregularity in our movements soon caused the whole beach to become a sea of craning necks, like thick swaying snakes, and their barking usually increased in volume. If we froze in our tracks, they soon settled down again and they didn't seem to acknowledge us at all if we remained in the tree line.

Although it was exciting to be so close to these huge creatures, we always bore in mind the fate of a scientist who approached too close to an adult male sea-lion. The animal, startled by the close proximity of the man, suddenly arched back and bit him on his backside with such force that he was unable to walk for days!

We noticed that some of the older animals had a yellowish growth

Humpback whale in Fredrick Sound (Photo Duncan Richards)

Sealion beach on the Brothers Island

on their coats, which was actually a fungus. Sea-lions do not moult and have one coat from birth to death. Living in a constantly damp environment this fungus often takes hold on the skins of older animals and this leads to rotting of the skin and eventually death. A similar thing happens to bears. They do not moult and if they hibernate in a cave with a constant drip, a fungus develops on their skin and this eventually kills them.

Towards the end of the day we fished for halibut and after losing a few herrings and a couple of hooks, we managed to land a good sized one. Halibut bite quickly but put up a good fight and often break the line.

Just before bed, we made an adventurous approach towards the sea-lion beach by kayak. They accepted our presence until we crossed the invisible line that marked their territory. In a flash, dozens of them took to the water and drove us away with their intimidating barks and sheer numbers. A friend of ours had to defend himself from a belligerent sea-lion, when he canoed too close to its harem, by jabbing his paddle into the animal's mouth.

During the mating season, they approach small boats that encroach on their territorial boundaries and occasionally they even bump against the boats, open their mouths to display their teeth, bark loudly and blow nasal mucus in order to frighten the trespassers away.

Luckily, we only had an enthusiastic posse of young males hounding us away, but they followed us closely and barked loudly until we were well away from their beach. When they had gone, we drifted back to our camp on the tide, relieved that the sea-lions did not convert our intrusion into a wet experience. In the shallow water, we drifted over thousands of sea urchins and starfish, before landing for another bear-free night.

Day 99 21st July

The day started well with a high tide which meant a minimal boat carry. It was also the third consecutive day without rain and all our gear was bone dry.

We paddled past the 'sea-lion' beach for the last time, and began a 25 mile journey along the southern shore of Admiralty Island. Recognising the island's reputation for bears, we decided to cover as much ground as possible, to avoid camping for more than one or two nights. Our destination was a small island in Herring Bay, about three-quarters of the way along the south end of the island. It was the only island along the entire coast that looked reasonably well located to minimize the bear hazard of a main island camp.

The entire coastline was very rocky and steep, and the forest grew in a lush green tangle which overflowed the menacing, black cliffs. The thought of canoeing twenty five miles was daunting, particularly as we both felt weak and lethargic.

We could see our destination in the far distance, almost from the time we set off, and consequently the twenty five miles passed very slowly. Kris became very tired and had a little cry, but we pressed on and eventually arrived in Herring Bay, having stopped only once to replenish our water supply from a wide salmon stream.

Our proposed island camp site was disappointing, as it was connected to the main island by a short peninsular, that was only covered for about an hour at high tide.

We lacked the energy and inclination to paddle to the next island, so camp was set up on a comfortable site and Kris soon had a fire going. Smoke from our fire attracted three fishermen, who rowed over to us from their fishing boat moored in the bay. We chatted for a while and they gave us a dozen eggs and some beer for good luck. They had sailed all the way from Seattle for the salmon season, and they estimated that two-thirds of the boats fishing in Alaska at that time were from the lower forty-eight States. They up-dated us with the local and international news and invited us to visit their boat in the morning to collect a couple of salmon.

Soon after they had left, Krista went to bed and was soon asleep. I quietly finished the packing and secured the kayaks for the night.

Once the chores were done, I sat alone next to the fire and watched the dusk descend peacefully on the water. Suddenly, I spotted two huge, dark brown bears and a cub ambling along the beach towards us, and they appeared to be walking directly towards the peninsular that connected our island to the mainland. I leapt to my feet and threw a handful of greenery on the flames to make the fire smoke. Our pots and pans were all packed, so I could not rattle them. Instinctively, I grabbed a brittle piece of wood we had collected for the fire, and snapped it. The sharp crack startled the bears and they shuffled off into the forest. Somewhat relieved, I waited quietly to see if they would come back. They did! They re-emerged from the forest and were now much nearer our camp. I broke another stick and ran to wake Krista, scanning the forest all the time for suitable trees to climb, as a last resort.

Krista was up in a flash and, in record time, we had the tent down and ourselves installed in the kayaks. The bears were far too close for comfort, and they gave us the necessary motivation to embark on our first night paddle!

Darkness fell as we left the island and an overcast sky created an extra dark night. All we could see of the land was a dark, black mass which we kept on our right hand side. We could not see each other at all, except for odd moments when the moon found some thin cloud to shine through, so we kept within ear-shot of each other's paddle strokes.

Our only light came from the electric blue and green specks of phosphorescence, that shone like flickering stars in the water agitated by our paddles. It was the brightest phosphorescence I had ever seen, and it kept us hypnotised as we paddled steadily onwards.

The lights of a fishing boat moved slowly towards us, with its search-light scanning the shore and illuminating the trees in its moving beam. As it drew nearer, the crew failed to see us and they crossed our bows dangerously close.

About two hours after leaving camp, we managed to find the next island but to our dismay it was bordered by steep, crumbly and un-climbable cliffs. Our options were now seriously narrowed; we could either paddle until daybreak or sleep on the mainland. We were both desperately tired so we decided to try and land. Rocks were impossible to see and we bumped and scraped over several before finding ourselves on a small beach.

With the aid of a dim torch, we collected enough wood for a fire and then checked the area for bear sign. Fortunately the wood was dry and we were soon enjoying a roaring fire. The thought of sleeping on a dark beach on Admiralty Island, especially after our recent bear sightings, made us reluctant to sleep, so we decided that one of us should try to stay awake and keep watch.

I volunteered for the first stint and by 4am Krista was asleep with her head resting on my lap. I soon lost interest in keeping watch and fell asleep as well, waking only once to extinguish my burning clothes.

Dawn broke at 5.30am and we were pleased to be in one piece. Our clothes were covered in burn and melt marks from red hot embers and my foot was firmly lodged in a substantial pile of fresh bear scat! Whether the droppings had been deposited while I was asleep, or whether I had deposited my foot on it, we couldn't decide. We did know that a bear had been in the area very recently.

Numbed by fatigue, we ignored it and dozed for a few more hours next to the fire, feeling a little safer in the daylight.

Day 100 22nd July

At about 9am we sorted ourselves out and paddled, in a trance, away from the beach. In the very next bay, two hefty bears rummaged amongst the driftwood.

A cluster of fishing boats jostled for position at Gardner Point, at the south-westerly tip of Admiralty Island, as we started the five mile crossing of Chatham Strait and we were pleased to leave Admiralty Island behind us.

At midday we landed at a small boulder-strewn beach on Baranof Island. Dry wood was abundant and we soon had a good cooking fire under way. The 'Observer' charter boat, we had met three days earlier, steamed past about a mile away and, to our surprise, the boat turned and came towards us. They had seen the smoke from our fire and had assumed that it was a distress signal. 'After all,' joked the Captain, 'you wouldn't normally be in a place like that unless you were in distress.'

After a cup of tea and a kip, we aimed our kayaks northwards and paddled the three miles to the enticingly named inlet of Warm Springs Bay. The bay was a mile and a half deep and was headed by a majestically pounding waterfall. It also had its own resident grey whale. Near the waterfall was a cluster of wooden cabins and a floating dock. Several sailing boats and some fishing boats lay bobbing on the rippling sea and, in the middle, holding pride of place on the dock was the good ship 'Observer'. As we drew alongside, the crew invited us for supper that evening and we readily accepted.

The village of Baranof had as its centre a two-storey, creosoted building, which was built on stilts next to the jetty. It served as shop and home for the proprietor, whose name was Wally. He had established a 'Warm Bath' business, by piping natural hot spring water from the hills, to a small hut which housed several metal bath tubs. We were both in dire need of a bath, so we opted for a romantic soak in one of Wally's larger tubs. We bought a six pack of beer in preparation, and leapt in the soothing water. Unfortunately, our long, relaxing bath came to an abrupt end when Krista, overcome by the heat, leapt out of the bath and vomitted out of the window. I was at a loss to know what to do, so I did the gentlemanly thing, and drank her beer before it became too warm.

Two things struck us about Wally. His fanatical fascination for firearms and his enormous respect for bears. His latter quirk earned us a bed for the night as he did not relish the idea of us camping unarmed in his village.

A superb evening meal on the 'Observer', followed by a dry and comfortable bed in Wally's house, was a real boost for our physical and mental well being, especially after the excitement of the previous night.

Day 101   23rd July

We were more than impressed with Baranof village, so we decided to have a rest from canoeing and to have a walk in the surrounding hills. We stopped at the top of the 150ft waterfall for a close up of the pounding water and then continued to Baranof Lake, a mile further on. The lake water was like glass and we found a good beach in the shade of some trees. Most of the trees in the area were stunted and well spaced, and this afforded superb views of the islands, bays and mountains in the area.

As we sat by the lake, the tranquillity of the moment was shattered by the sound of loud disco music. At first it was a faint background noise but it soon increased in volume, until its source was revealed in the shape of two buxom women with a 'ghetto blaster'. Many Alaskans take music when they walk in the hills so as to warn animals of their presence. These two ladies also sported Magnum 44 hand guns just in case of trouble!

After a few hours of pleasant walking we returned to Baranof and mended some minor holes in the kayaks and then chatted with Wally. He was the only Baranof resident who lived there the whole year round, and he keeps his house warm in winter by using the hot spring water in his radiators.

Wally is one of S.E. Alaska's characters and he has had an interesting but turbulent past. Much of his time had been spent fighting in South and Central America as a mercenary, which accounted for his abnormal interest in guns. Dozens of them were housed on his walls and, to pass the time of day, he regularly discharged hot lead into nearby trees. He made his own ammunition and everywhere you looked in his house there were weapons or piles of cartridges.

On his front door was a sign that read, 'We're insured by Smith and Wesson' and on the store counter two bear skulls were exhibited. One of the bears had been shot, from the hip, from twelve feet when a friend had startled a bear feeding on a deer carcass. 'Had to change his underwear before returning to pick it up,' quipped Wally. 'The other,' Wally explained, 'had forgotten to hibernate because the winter that year had been exceptionally mild.' Apparently, some of the late sleepers became hungry and wandered down to the sea and one had crawled

123

under Wally's house to eat the mussels that grew on the support piles. Unfortunately, the bear pushed some of the piles over first, so Wally shot it before his house collapsed in the sea.

Wally's advice on bears was unending. He warned, 'Lady bears dig tunnels uphill to protect the cubs in winter; man bears dig horizontal tunnels and dumb-ass bears dig them downhill. When it rains, the snow melts and the bears wake up cold and wet. If a bear wakes up pissed off, he stays that way for the rest of the year!!'

His advice on what to do if a bear attacked was 'Fire a flare at it and catch his whiskers alight. They don't like that.' Wally's last two dogs were taken by bears, and he thinks it is tempting fate to go into the forest without a rifle.

One story we heard about Wally that is worth a mention happened when a rowdy crew of drunk fishermen descended on Baranof Warm Springs. They had a bath, and then stole all Wally's towels. They returned to their boat closely followed by Wally who politely asked for his towels back. This request was met by a hail of verbal abuse, so he sauntered back to his house. A while later he opened the window of his top room and shouted 'Give me my towels back, or else.' The abuse flowed again, so Wally 'let them have it' with his submachine gun. He strafed the mast and rigging of their boat, and magically the towels flew out of the hatches on to the dock.

Day 102 24th July

Due to the comfort of Wally's house, we were late to rise the next morning and during a hearty breakfast of fish, he proudly showed us his latest stock of ammunition.

Shortly after midday we said 'goodbye' and paddled into a stiff breeze past the whale at the mouth of the bay. We turned north into Chatham Strait, up the last long strait of our trip. It lead into Icy Strait which, for us, was the gateway to Glacier Bay.

We camped on a small rock called Takatz Island, which offered a commanding view of the route ahead of us.

Day 103 25th July

There was very little wind, and we paddled on a colourful sea until lunchtime, when we stopped a short distance from a 400ft high waterfall, that thundered straight into the sea. The surroundings were so pleasant that we spent a couple of hours over lunch, watching the teeming life in the crystal-clear sea. Salmon leapt nearby, and shoals of minute fish swam in droves between the seaweed and the shallows.

The past few days of relaxation had worked wonders for us, and we were both feeling a little more human after the rigours of the last 100 days of canoeing and camping. The map showed a cabin on Crow Island, so we decided to camp there. On landing, however, we found that it had been crushed by a fallen tree, and all that remained was a pile of rotted wood.

Day 104 26th July

We left Crow Island, and paddled straight into a fast tide. The point we were aiming for, was only two miles away, but it took over 1½ hours to get there. The water reared up into steep breaking waves, that took us by surprise and threatened to capsize us. Where the water calmed, we were greeted by a playful sextet of otters, who were enjoying the wind and tide. From a safe distance they watched us paddle around the point, and into Chatham Strait, before disappearing from view.

We were in an odd tidal area here, as both the flood and ebb tides go against us. Normally, in a long strait the flood travels one way, and the ebb the other, meaning that for six hours during the day the tide helps with forward progress.

At lunchtime we landed on an open stony beach, with a green border of alder bushes between us and the forest. Krista's eyes lit up at the opportunity for a squat in the bushes, and off she went to find a prime spot.

A few minutes later she emerged from the trees with an expression of horror on her face. She had found a pile of bones, with a pair of training shoes next to them. The bones were well weathered and the shoes sprouting moss. We assumed the worse, but on closer inspection, we realised that the bones were too large to be human remains, and that they were probably those of a bear. There was no skull, which suggested that the bear had been shot by hunters, (all skulls must be submitted to the Fish and Game Department) so we could only speculate as to how the shoes got there - was it a bear victim, or maybe a practical joke? If it was a joke, the chance of anyone finding the bones was extremely remote. The nearest settlement was over 50 miles away, and the coast was only accessible to small craft.

After lunch, we left our bizarre find behind, and continued our battle against the tide, finally pulling on to a rough pebble beach on Fairway Island, mid-way across Peril Strait.

Day 105 27th July

We paddled against the tide most of the day, before landing to camp on the vast island of Chicagof. It had been a long slog of a day and we were knackered. Chatham Strait was too long, wide and straight to be interesting but we did notice that the leaves were turning yellow, a sure indication that summer was coming to an end already.

Day 106 28th July

In the early hours we were woken by the scuffing sound of an animal padding through the forest towards us. We both froze with terror, and I whispered, 'stay still whatever you do.' It was obvious that the animal was heavy, and the sound of its paws was accompanied by strange asthmatic breathing and intermittent snuffles. It walked slowly past Krista's side of the tent, sniffing all the time. We whispered softly to each other, to let it know that something was inside, and at the same time tried not to startle it. It gradually worked its way past the end of the tent, and then ambled off towards the sea. The thing that puzzled us about the unknown animal was that it leapt into the water with a tremendous splash, and that was the last we heard of it! From the darkness of the tent our imaginations ran riot, so we snuggled up, but didn't manage to sleep after that.

Krista was exceptionally tired, and a little jumpy all day. This was not surprising - she hasn't been sleeping at all well lately! We paddled eighteen miles today, spurred on by the thought of reaching Tenakee Springs village.

About five miles short of the village we stopped on a beach for a rest, and almost succumbed to camping there but the distant town was tantalisingly close, so we paddled on. This was just as well because, looking back at our beach, we saw a large brown bear running along the sand at a fast but graceful lope.

At Tenakee Springs we moored to the visitors' jetty, and erected the tent in a nearby forest clearing. There was bear scat everywhere, but we felt strangely safe camping near a village.

Krista takes a rest

The Mysterious bones and training shoes

An exploratory stroll revealed that Tenakee Springs stretched for about half a mile along a solitary unmetalled track. On each side of the track were wooden houses; some ramshackle and others built of freshly-cut pine. Sea-faring artefacts hung from some of the houses, and the only motorised transport seemed to be small three-wheeled motor cycles. At the main crossroads where the fishing jetty met the track, hung an artificial set of traffic lights. From the end of the jetty we could see that most of the dwellings on the seaward side of the track, were built on stilts. We visited the local store and bought some food, to give our taste buds a change from fish and lentil stew.

Straight after the meal we hit the sack and fell asleep surprisingly quickly, considering the profusion of bear droppings in the area!

Day 107   29th July

It was a shockingly late hour when we poked our dishevelled heads out of the tent and got up.

After a quick breakfast, I walked along the track to sample the delights of the warm springs. Tenakee villagers lacked somewhat in sporting instincts, because men and women had separate times for using the springs, with a 'safe' period of a few minutes between. The bathing times for each sex were worked out evenly, with certain periods during the day for everyone. There was, however, a local battle raging amongst the townspeople of Tenakee Springs. The women wanted more hours, because 'we need more time in the bath than men.'

The bath house was a square, grey concrete building maintained by the locals. A door led from the changing area to a sunken cuboid room that was lit by a small skylight. The walls and floor were of drab, grey concrete, and the centrepiece of the steamy room was a six feet square pool of beautifully clear water. The pool was about six feet deep and the hot water bubbled up from a crack between two boulders. Detergents were not allowed in the spring and, around the room, plastic containers were provided for scooping water, and rinsing off the soap. I spent an enjoyable half-hour soaking in the hot water and while I was there, I met Bob and Jay, a fisherman and his nephew. He told me that his boat was moored to the visitors' jetty, and that we would be welcome to visit them later.

After the bath, Krista and I decided to take a stroll along the 'Tenakee Recreational Footpath'. A large sign warned us of bears, and fresh bear droppings lay on the path. Bears were obviously nearby, but we decided not to let that spoil our walk.

A short way along the forest path another couple were walking a few hundred yards ahead of us. Our pace was faster than theirs and we gradually closed the gap between us. When we were approximately fifty feet behind them, one of us trod on a twig, making a sharp crack. At once they spun round with a look of sheer terror on their faces, and levelled a gun in our direction. On seeing us they sighed with relief and shouted, 'Don't ever do that again to someone with a loaded Magnum 44.' They were obviously extremely jumpy, and I wondered to myself what was more dangerous, walking in bear country unarmed, or having a forest full of nervous people with loaded guns!

A little further along the path a large brown bear barred our way, and stood facing us. It was dark chocolate brown in colour, and, on all fours, stood about four feet high at the shoulder. It acknowledged our presence and we just stood and stared at each other. The couple with the gun soon caught us up and after a minute or two, the bear sauntered off into the forest.

The couple decided to take a photograph, so one adopted a 'Starsky and Hutch' pose, with his gun levelled across his forearm, while the other muttered repeatedly, 'keep me covered.' We witnessed the amusing spectacle for a while and then left them to it. The bear had disappeared and, in any case, their gun manners did little to inspire confidence.

The brown bear was a magnificent animal, more powerful than the black bear, and certainly more worthy of respect.

Back at the boats we were just about to start a fish and chips supper, when Bob turned up with his lady partner, Dodie. They invited us aboard their boat and offered to take us fishing at the mouth of the Tenakee Inlet. We accepted enthusiastically and, over coffee, they suggested that we slept in their house in a proper bed.

Our kayaks were tied behind their boat and off we went, leaving the stilted frontage of Tenakee Springs behind us. The 'Mayflower' had a chronic list to starboard, caused by the fish being loaded to one side, but this did not seem to worry Bob. Gradually, a chop built up on the sea and the fishing tackle clinked in time with the waves. Our kayaks began battering against each other and almost turning over as they hit each wave. Not wishing to lose our gear, we mentioned the fact to Bob. 'No problem,' he said, 'we'll haul them aboard.' With considerable effort, we heaved them on to the already cramped deck and continued on our way.

The chosen fishing spot was the current at the mouth of the inlet, and Dodie set about winching down the long wooden spreaders, while Bob set the lines. The two lines were weighted with lead cannon balls, and lowered into the sea with a trail of assorted hooks and lures trolling behind. The wooden spreaders forced the lines apart to avoid tangling, and the boat was set on a wide circular course. Within a few minutes of lowering the lines, the spreaders twitched furiously and Bob wound in the first salmon. He drew it expertly alongside the vessel and hooked it out of the water with a well aimed gaff hook. No sooner had he got it aboard, the line was re-set and he commenced gutting and cleaning the fish.

During the few hours we spent fishing, the bites came thick and fast. We hauled in Coho, humpback and King Salmon as well as a few halibut. Halibut was out of season, so they were tossed back into the sea, as were King Salmon that were under 28″ in length. Anything under 28″ was considered a tiddler and couldn't be sold! Trolling was the technique used to catch good quality fish. It was a much slower process than dropping a seine net or trawling, but the money gained for undamaged fish more than compensated for what they lost in bulk.

We soon got the hang of it and got stuck into setting the lines and gutting the fish. Trolling proved to be hard work but it did give us an insight into the life of an Alaskan fisherman.

At nightfall we packed up the lines, hung up the lures, and chugged away from the inlet mouth towards their home in Cedar Cove.

Bob sells his salmon for 3.25 dollars per pound, and in the shops, even in Alaska, it retailed at 6 dollars per pound.

We motored along for several hours through the night, in waters that were obviously familiar to Bob, until about 2am when, with the aid of a powerful searchlight, we squeezed between two islands into Cedar Cove.

Bob and Dodies's house was built on floating logs, and the fishing boat was tied up alongside. We were soon inside, and everyone disappeared to their appropriate beds. Bob, Dodie and Jay slept in the boat, whilst we kipped in the house. The heating was on and we slept well, despite the occasional face full of moulting cat!

Day 108 30th July

In the light of day the house was revealed to us. It was a small, one-roomed house, that was heated by a home-made wood burning stove that was fashioned from a 44 gallon oil drum, with a chimney of metal piping. It was remarkably efficient, and the house could be kept at sauna temperature with careful stoking. They had purchased the building five years previously for fifty dollars, from a cannery that went bust. They then slid it down the beach on to a wooden raft, and towed it behind the fishing boat to Cedar Cove. Since then improvements had been made and a tool shed added. The shed was crammed full with tools of every description and a wide variety of traps.

Bob fishes in the summer and traps for fur and meat in the winter. They enjoy their life at Cedar Cove, but did admit that the winter months were rather harsh. The snow quickly builds up and regular roof shovelling jaunts have to be made to prevent the house from sinking. They buy in bulk for the winter months and 200lbs of flour and 150lbs of potatoes usually sees them through.

Dodie prepared a huge fisherman's breakfast with several pints of coffee to accompany it. They were leaving for Juneau later that day to sell their fish and they offered to take us with them. The offer was tempting but we had our sights on Glacier Bay. Our day with Bob and Dodie had been an eye-opening experience for us and, with a degree of envy for their life style, we waved them 'goodbye.'

They chugged out of Cedar Cove still waving heartily whilst we paddled the short distance to Cedar Island, where Dodie had her vegetable patch. We spent the afternoon sleeping and in the evening we devoured huge helpings of salmon before crashing out for an early night.

Day 109 31st July

The tide rose higher than expected during the night and washed away our cooking pot, mugs, cutlery and spatula. On self-contained expeditions such as ours spares are not carried, and the loss of the smallest piece of equipment can be extremely inconvenient. We searched along the beach in both directions, and soon came to realise that our only cooking pot had gone for ever.

The canoeing started with a four mile dog-leg to round the end of the slender Iyoukeen Peninsular. Once round the point our course turned north again, and we hit an icy north wind head on. Two hours later and in great need of rest, we aimed for the shore, and two hump backs passed close to us, providing a pleasant surprise. On windy days humpbacks are more difficult to see, because their backs blend in with the dark waves, and the spumes disperse instantly in the wind. The sound of crashing waves also overwhelms the tell-tale sound of exhalation, that on calm days can be heard for miles.

A roaring fire soon took the chill out of our bones, and we ate some of Bob's salmon.

Later in the day the wind calmed and we pressed on, stopping only

131

to fill our water bottles. Two young deer drank from the same stream, and their casual manner indicated that no bears were in the vicinity.

Camp that night was on the mainland Chichagof Island in a steep-sided cove.

I found a deer antler, and Krista discovered a method of removing maggots from the berries we pick. Put the berries in a bowl of seawater, and the maggots float to the top!

Day 110 1st August

It was a clear bright day, and we managed to cover twenty miles against the tide. Since staying with Wally at Baranof Warm Springs, we had been slogging up the wide, never-ending Chatham Strait but today we turned out of it, giving us a sudden change of scenery. A hundred miles away, the snow-covered peaks of the Fairweather Range reared above the deep blue waters of Icy Strait, soaring to heights in excess of 15,000 ft. The Fairweather Range combine with the St Elias Mountains to form the highest coastal range in the world. The highest peak being Mount St. Elias, that reaches 18,008 ft.

Nowadays, Icy Strait is rarely icy, but its name dates from 1794, when Capt. George Vancouver was exploring the area in search of the North West Passage. In his day the strait was choked with icebergs from a huge glacier which, over the centuries has receded, revealing Glacier Bay as we know it today.

The wildlife of Icy Strait was out in force and we saw whales, porpoises, sea-lions, deer and hundreds of leaping salmon.

We pulled up on Puluzzi Island for the night, and camped with a clear view of the distant mountains. On the beach we found a cooking pot, bigger and better than the one we had lost, and inside was a spoon!

It had been a great day, and our morale was high.

Day 111 2nd August

Another beautiful clear day greeted us, and we paddled five miles into the navy blue waters of Icy Strait. The paddle across was leisurely and we soaked up the sun, drank in the views, and tried to catch some fish. Close to the island I hooked a good sized halibut - ideal for two hungry people.

The site was too good to leave in a hurry, so we lay out on the beach,

Krista fishing in Icy Strait

A peaceful campsite in S.E. Alaska

and made the most of that rare S.E. Alaskan commodity; sunshine. A dip in the sea confirmed that Icy Strait lived up to its name, but in the sunshine we soon recovered. The tree line on the mainland was now down to 4,000 ft with most of the hills being bare-topped, indicating recent glacial activity.

Day 112 3rd August

We breakfasted on the remains of the fish we caught yesterday, and then paddled away across the last four miles of Icy Strait. It was another glorious day, and we revelled in the views. The Fairweather mountains appeared slightly hazier than yesterday, but the white snow and vertical rock bands stood out in sharp relief.

Dozens of propoises swam lazily on the surface, often in pairs, and whispering abruptly each time they broke surface. Although more salmon were leaping here, they still managed to elude our fishing tackle and after fourteen miles of trawling, we failed to trap a fish. We were not too worried because we hoped to reach a town tomorrow, and that meant a new supply of fresh food.

Early in the afternoon we arrived on the aptly-named Porpoise Island, and dragged the kayaks up the steep shingle beach. This suited us because we gained height to the high tide mark quickly, without the effort of a long gradual carry.

The island had an abundant supply of firewood and looked relatively animal-free, but it was the discovery of wild peas and strawberries that convinced us that we had hit on an excellent camping spot.

Day 113 4th August

To make sure that the day ran with maximum efficiency we rose early and, to save time, ate a pre-prepared breakfast.

We were heading for the town of Gustavus, where we planned to pick up our final food cache for the last part of our journey into the Glacier Bay National Monument. From experience, we knew that on Saturdays Post Offices shut at midday, so we had to get there on time.

Although the sunshine of the last few days had gone, the morning was calm and we arrived at Gustavus Pier at 9.30am. We hauled the kayaks on to the float jetty at the end of the pier, changed into our jeans, and climbed the overhanging ladder on to the pier itself. It stretched for 100 yards over flat sand, linking the deep water of Icy Pass to the road. A dirt road disappeared into the distance and Gustavus was nowhere to be seen.

Two fishermen drove on to the pier and wished us good luck for the walk to the Post Office. The time was actually 8.30am because we had forgotten to set our watches to Alaskan time. In the past Alaska was divided into time zones, but Government offices could not operate efficiently, so Alaska was turned into a one-time zone, purely to alleviate bureaucratic hassle. Consequently in S.E. Alaska dusk and dawn are an hour earlier than they should be.

On the three mile walk to the Post Office, we only passed a few houses. The Post Office was housed in an old barrack hut painted light blue and, on the door a notice announced that it opened at 2pm on Saturdays!

We had five hours to kill, so we decided to do the rest of our shopping. The only problem was that Gustavus store was about two miles from the Post Office! The store was a pink caravan, and we arrived to find that it was shut all weekend.

Our next plan was to find a café in which to sit to escape the drizzle which was now falling. The coffee shop was a mile further on from the store and it was open but we were shattered to find that it was a hotel, and was closed to non-residents! Feeling dejected, but faintly amused, we walked back to the kayaks for a pancake session.

Several hours later and fortified by a warming dose of stodge, we retraced the three miles to Gustavus Post Office. The town of Gustavus consisted of about twenty houses, spread over an area of 100 square miles, and all linked by dirt roads.

At the Post Office we had a stack of letters from home, but to our dismay the elderly postmistress was adamant that no food boxes had arrived for us. We were in dire straits without them, so I invited myself to the other side of the counter to make a search. I eventually found them under a pile of more recently delivered goods.

Carrying the heavy awkward boxes back to the boats proved to be a trial of endurance, but after a struggle we made it with arms six inches longer than when we started!

As we packed, some fishermen pulled up at the jetty with a 180lb halibut aboard their boat. It towered above its burly 6ft captor, who posed proudly next to it. It was difficult to try and imagine the size of a 700 pounder, but easy to understand how fishermen had been killed in the holds of their boats by the flapping of a Pacific halibut.

We camped on the sand that night, and the main hazard came from a noisy beach party who decided, in their drunken state, to practice handbrake turns, in their pickup truck, near our tent.

GLACIER BAY , ALASKA

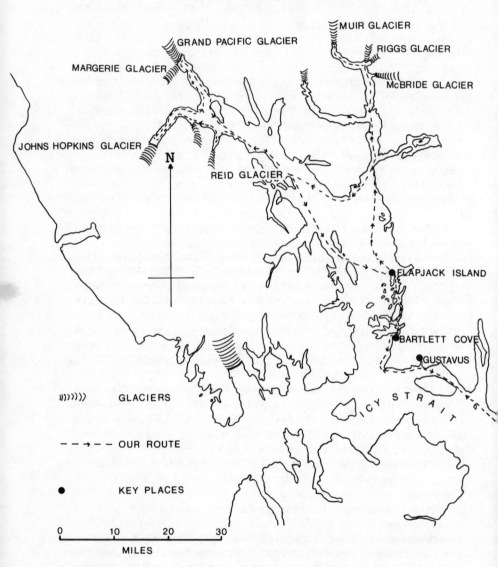

MUIR GLACIER

RIGGS GLACIER

GRAND PACIFIC GLACIER

McBRIDE GLACIER

MARGERIE GLACIER

JOHNS HOPKINS GLACIER

N

REID GLACIER

FLAPJACK ISLAND

BARTLETT COVE

GUSTAVUS

ICY STRAIT

))))))) GLACIERS

– – –→– – OUR ROUTE

● KEY PLACES

0   10   20   30
MILES

Glacier Bay showing our route

Chapter Seven: **Bay of White Thunder**

Day 114 5th August

The mist and drizzle of yesterday had vanished, and in the clear blue sky the Fairweather range loomed dramatically nearer.

For the first hour after leaving Gustavus, our course followed a long sandy beach directly towards the snow-covered mountains until, six miles further on, the entrance to Glacier Bay opened up before us, and we swung northwards into it.

Immediately the water changed colour and temperature. It was as calm as a mill pond, and the air was filled with the sound of hundreds of sea birds. It was almost like canoeing over a polished frosted glass surface.

Amongst the gulls, oyster catchers and muralets, we saw our first puffins flying, with very little grace, in large circles overhead.

The entrance to the bay was a hive of activity, bordered by a magnificent amphitheatre of high white mountains. Glacier Bay is a National Monument, and all human activities centred around one hotel and a Ranger Station in Bartlett Cove. Our plan was to camp at Bartlett Cove for a few days of rest, before heading into the bay itself.

At Bartlett Cove we met other canoeists who were on a two weeks holiday and they directed us towards the campsite. Access to Glacier Bay is only possible by air or sea, so consequently it was prohibitively expensive to get there without your own transport. The Glacier Bay Lodge Hotel proved to be very expensive. A shower, for example, cost £2. A qualification for a typical hotel guest was to be excessively paranoid about bears, and one even told us that we must have a subconscious death wish to want to camp! One of the kayakers we met at Bartlett Cove worked as an assistant Ranger for the summer, and in the evening we were invited for a meal, a beer and a free shower.

Day 115 6th August

Today was devoted to rest and recuperation, and the highlight came when a middle-aged couple from New York wandered over to see what we were cooking. They were so shocked at the sight of our charcoal chips swimming in murky oil that they invited us out for a meal! The offer was too good to refuse, and, that evening we dined in the Guest House at Gustavus.

The meal was excellent - a whole salmon each, garnished with an enormous salad. Conversation at the table was dominated by a loud, arrogant and obscenely rich Mormon couple, who boasted about themselves to anyone within earshot. The New Yorkers, however, were a very hospitable couple and we enjoyed the evening and their company immensely.

It was pouring with rain when we left, the dirt road had become a quagmire and we had a ten mile walk back towards Bartlett Cove. In the darkness we managed five miles before a vehicle gave us a lift for the rest of the way. The pickup truck was described by the driver as 'a typical Gustavus vehicle; unlicensed and unroadworthy, but who cares in Gustavus - there are only ten miles of road.'

Day 116 7th August

Krista went shopping in Gustavus but could only buy sugar-free chocolate (just what we need!) and mushy onions. In the evening a bar session, with a local Tlingit Indian, put the dampers on our third attempt at an early night.

Day 117 8th August

It was another wet day, so we got up late, washed our clothes and prepared food for our departure into the bay. Much of the day was spent bundled by a fire at the camp site, chatting to a couple of Swedish film makers, whose filming of a T.V. documentary had been rained off for a few days.

At last we succeeded in our quest for an early night!

Day 118 9th August

The expedition into Glacier Bay kicked off on a dreary, wet day. We paddled for twelve miles through the flat, thickly forested, and relatively uninteresting Beardslee Islands, coming finally to rest on the small lump of Flapjack Island.

As the tide ebbed in the evening, Flapjack Island increased to about 10 times its original size, and became the feeding ground for hundreds of sea birds.

Picking wild peas and strawberries kept us off the streets in the evening, until three killer whales diverted our attention by swimming past very close to the shore. We followed them on foot, but their head start was too much for us to catch up with them. As always, the sight of these creatures was exciting, and our attempt at running beside them had at least exercised our legs. We were lulled to sleep by the continual sound of barking seals.

Day 119 10th August

The wind and tide slowed us down to an average speed of two knots and, in a cold hanging mist, we set out on a six mile crossing to South Marble Island. Halfway across the mist thickened, blocking out all sight of land. Keeping on a vague course with the compass, half an hour passed before the outline of the island returned into view. The crossing took twice as long as expected and, using the now visible island as a reference, we realised that a strong tide had been flowing against us.

The smooth, rocky mounds of the Marble Islands were natural bird rookeries. They were remote in location, totally free of land predators, and even man would experience extreme difficulty in landing on the steep sided rock.

Realising the safety of this natural haven, hundreds of birds use it each year for nesting and rearing their young. Bonaparte gulls, oyster catchers, grebes, guillemots and horned puffins were all very much in evidence, perched on every conceivable ledge and crevice. The air was alive with the sound of birds, and some of the large gulls warned us away with low flying aerobatics.

In the mist and wind we became very cold, and, for the first time since the beginning of the trip, we had to wear our hats and thermal underwear. The wind was unrelenting, so soon after leaving the Marble Islands, we aimed our boats towards Sturgess Island, some five miles away and set up camp.

Day 120 11th August

During the night the wind increased to storm level, and buffeted the tent violently. The pegs weren't very secure, so to make sure the tent would still be there in the morning, we had to get up during the night and anchor them down with rocks.

The storm forced us to lie-in, and we ended up spending the entire day on Sturgess Island.

On the mainland, opposite our island, was Sandy Cove, the scene of a bear fatality three years ago. The bear was still considered to be aggressive, and visitors to Glacier Bay are warned not to go there. The animal has been known to shred rucksacks with its teeth and claws, in its attempt to rid the cove of what it considers to be threatening objects. Since the fatality, four other bears have been sighted in the area, suggesting that the attack was probably in defence of its young.

The wind died down in the evening and at dusk, as we lay asleep in the tent, we were woken by a terrifying roar. The noise was deep and bellowing and sounded very close to the tent. There was obviously a large creature outside and all we could do was lay still and silent to avoid startling it into aggression.

The growling continued, slowly and rhythmically and as far as we could tell, the animal was stationary. From our helpless position inside the flimsy orange shelter we imagined the worst and listened terrified as the horrific growling noise continued outside.

Several long minutes passed, so to ease the apparent stalemate, we cautiously manoeuvered to the entrance of the tent in the hope of catching a glimpse of the beast.

Kris quietly unzipped the tent door and with a huge sigh of relief we set eyes upon it.

It was a humpback whale snoring close to shore.

Day 121   12th August

Heavy rain during the night created a wet patch in the tent, which in turn destroyed all possibilities of sleep.

Paddling was uncomfortable in the biting wind and, as we struggled north toward Muir Point, we passed Garforth Island. We didn't see the famous Garforth bear that had been shot in the backside by a Ranger, and ever since, has displayed its aggression towards man by swimming out to small craft. Around Muir Point lay our first glacier so we heaved the boats up on to the beach and followed a fast-flowing, metallic grey glacial river upstream. The banks gradually steepened and became loose, so we opted for the safer but more tiresome route through the dense alder brush. A mile or so inland from the beach the clouds lifted dramatically revealing huge looming glaciers that hung precariously to the rock, thousands of feet above us.

Dirt Glacier, the one we were walking towards, was still out of sight, obscured by the dripping wet tangle of alders. Walking through alder brush is more akin to caving than walking, because you cannot see very far ahead and every now and then you have to crawl, grovel and contort to negotiate the branches. Ahead of us to the right a forty-five degree slope of sand and stone stretched out above the brush, so we struck towards that, hoping for relief from the undergrowth. Ten more minutes of scrummaging brought us to the bank where, panting and wet, we stood and gawped at the glacier before us.

It was a real let-down. No wonder they call it Dirt Glacier! Hardly a shred of ice was visible, just a vast pile of rubble stretching up the valley. After a few minutes the clouds dropped again, blotting out the hanging ice and leaving us with a view of what looked like a building site.

We turned around and reached the boats just in time to stop them from floating away on the tide, before paddling into Muir Inlet. Glacier Bay splits into a 'Y'-shape at Muir Point and Muir Inlet was the narrower right-hand fork.

The current flowing out of the inlet, and the cold wind from the ice, forced us to camp a few miles short of our intended destination and, from our campsite, through the faint mist, the striped winding form of Casement Glacier could be seen, stretching like a white three mile wide tongue from its high mountain source.

Today had been the fifth day of constant rain since entering the bay and it was playing havoc with morale. The wood was wet and, despite all our practice at firelighting, it took us two and a half hours to get a fire going. Every time it began to 'take' a large well placed drip dropped off a hood or sleeve and put the flame out with a sharp hiss.

Day 122   13th August

The morning continued cold and windy, but the clouds had risen significantly overnight, revealing the surrounding mountains, and giving a brighter, clearer view of Casement Glacier.

While we paddled, small ice lumps began appearing in the sea and the further up Muir Inlet we travelled, the more they increased in size and number, indicating our progress towards the glaciers.

By midday the grey skies gave way to blue, and shadows began to appear, focusing sharper as the sun brightened. The cold wind continued, but the day took on a much more cheerful and colourful hue. The icy water that, in the morning, had been a dull metallic grey was now almost unnatural blue, rather like an over touched-up postcard. The white form of Riggs Glacier fifteen miles distant shone clear white and looked very close. We noticed that since leaving Bartlett Cove the land had changed significantly. At the entrance to the bay, it was fairly flat and vegetated with a lush mature rain forest. About twenty miles further into the bay the rain forest was less apparent, and the land was covered mainly in a thick mass of alder bushes. Still further into the bay and a little closer to the glaciers, the coniferous trees became non-existent, and the alder began to thin out. Further still, the alders petered out almost completely, and the predominant plant life became the cotton topped dryas or mountain avon. The land nearest to the glaciers resembled a moonscape and was completely devoid of plant life.

In 1780 the glaciers of Glacier Bay, stretched right across the mouth of Icy Strait. By 1880 they had receeded over 30 miles freeing that land from its icy grip. Over the next hundred years it receded a further twenty miles into the bay, to where it is today. The retreat of the ice was dramatic, and there are few places in the world where the effects of a retreating ice age can be seen so vividly.

The plant recolonisation of the land is fascinating, and each stage we saw in reverse, while paddling up into the bay. Once the ice had retreated the earth was left sterile, and devoid of nutrients. The mountain avon spores then, spread on the wind, to gain the first foothold on the land and performed the vital function of introducing nitrogen into the earth. Soon afterwards the alder is able to grow in the form of small scrubby bushes in the newly fertilised land. Alder also induced nitrogen into the soil, and over the years it gradually overgrows the area, killing off the dryas by shutting out vital sunlight.

Meanwhile the glaciers retreat further, and the dryas follows in its path. Soon the land becomes fertile enough for the spruce and hemlock to germinate and take root. They grow fast and over the years kill off the alder in the same way that the alder destroyed the drayas, by light starvation. This is the birth of the rain forest and at the fringe of the forest where light is abundant, the alder still thrives creating a thick tangle for several yards before the forest floor opens out.

We stopped for lunch in a cove out of the wind, and ate an entire fruit cake. Our appetites seemed to be getting bigger than ever now with all the extra energy needed to stay warm. By evening we had arrived at Wolf Point only five miles short of our first glacier.

Leading from Wolf Point was the two thousand feet high White Thunder Ridge, so called because it used to be a prime viewing spot for calving glaciers before they retreated out of sight.

We walked about nine hundred feet up the ridge and actually

managed to work up a sweat. Our legs felt a bit feeble after a hundred and twenty days of not really using them, so we wimped out halfway along the ridge, and found a good view point for a sit down.

What we saw must have easily been the most spectacular sight of the trip.

Mountains soared up to seven thousand feet in all directions, all veined with white snow gullies leading to snow caked peaks. The sea, nine hundred feet below, was a deep turquoise blue flecked with small brilliant white icebergs, and between the far away hills surged grey glacial rivers.

The cold air made everything look doubly clear, and our route over the last two days in Muir Inlet could be traced and seen stretching away down the steep sided fjord.

In the far distance the mountains of Chicagof Island formed the horizon 90 miles away and it seemed amazing to think that we were there only ten days ago.

Day 123   14th August

We were woken up by the heat of the sun, and emerged from the tent to discover a perfectly still day. After eating breakfast on the ridge we took advantage of the calm weather, and paddled off across Muir Inlet to see McBride Glacier.

The tide was ebbing, so we pulled our boats up on to the shore, and left them lodged between some car-sized ice blocks, before walking beside a seething brown river that led us to McBride Glacier. The 'moonscape' of bare rocks was littered with large stranded lumps of ice that looked strangely out of place in this desert. Our walk weaved a course through the icebergs, and over mounds of loose rubble until three quarters of an hour later we arrived at the snout of McBride Glacier.

In front of us lay an area of water above which loomed a 200 foot face of ice. We found a rock to sit on, and just stared at the deep blue wall of ice in front of us, as if expecting it to do something.

A torrent of rubble-laden water surged powerfully from a cave beneath the glacier, making the water boil violently.

Every now and then the might of the glacier pushing from behind splintered the ice deep inside creating loud 'pistol' cracks. Straining against the moving mass, a towering column of white ice leaned precariously forward over the water, and we watched hoping to see it fall. We sat for over an hour, but nothing happened, so we hiked back to the kayaks before the tide had a chance to drift them away.

Back at the boats and over a mile away from the glacier a thunderous rumble echoed from its direction; we looked back, and saw that the ice pillar had toppled.

We soon launched again and headed further up the inlet towards the next glacier.

The white tongue of ice called Riggs Glacier forges its unstoppable path from the heights of the Takpinsha Mountains and ends at sea level as a wall of ice a mile and a half wide, and 160 feet high. The weight behind the ice is difficult to comprehend and, as with all glaciers in the bay, it is fuelled by an annual snowfall exceeding 2,000 inches. High in the mountains the snow doesn't melt and each year another 160 feet falls on top of the existing snow. Over the years the snow at the lower levels changes form under the incalculable weight above. Gradually it turns to ice, not the type you get in your freezer at home, but a much denser, harder and colder ice.

After several thousand years of perpetual snow build-up, gravity and the weight of the ice causes it to move downhill. From this moment a glacier is born. The snow keeps falling and the ice keeps moving until its melt rate equals the rate at which it is being fuelled. In its path it pushes and grinds away at the earth, forming deep valleys and drastically reshaping the earth.

Riggs Glacier, as with most of the others in Glacier Bay, was retreating slowly due to warmer climatic trends over the past few thousand years.

A retreating tide water glacier is a spectacular sight, because every now and then chunks of ice fall off into the sea. We watched and waited, but nothing happened and after a significant time-lapse we became more complacent, and inched closer to the ice wall. Plenty of small football-sized lumps tumbled into the sea with a surprisingly loud noise but we wanted to see a big one.

A sub-glacial river forged up from under the ice, creating an unpredictable current, so to avoid constant manoeuvering, we clung on to a grounded iceberg and waited.

Every now and then a loud splintering noise came from deep within the ice, signalling its imperceptable movement but nothing large collapsed.

After a while hunger got the better of us, and we retreated to shore. In the evening as we sat on the beach, a thunderous crash filled our ears and we looked up just in time to see a section of the 160 foot face collapse, seemingly in slow motion, into the sea. An explosive spray reared up, and lumps of ice the size of house bricks flew in all directions. As the spray subsided, a six foot wave appeared and spread in

Lazy day at Riggs Glacier

The snout of Lamplugh Glacier

a semi-circle away from the collapsed berg. Behind it smaller subsidiary waves followed. They tore through the grounded ice lumps that we had been resting on earlier, and rolled them over and over as if they were weightless. It washed up the cliff side in slow motion, and crashed its way through the ice towards us.

Suddenly it dawned on us that the boats were in danger, so we sprang to our feet and did the fastest boat carry on record up the beach! We threw our other equipment as far up the bank as possible, and then we waited for the wave to hit. It travelled the mile from the glacier to us in seconds, and washed up the beach to where we were standing. I held on to both boats as hard as possible to stop them from being wrenched from my grip, as the waves whooshed along the beach in front of us. Each one gradually became smaller, and after five minutes or so the sea was again calm, and the glacier looked innocent.

The only obvious changes in the scene were that the beach was now strewn with lumps of ice the size of household freezers, and a section of the glacier exposed more blue ice than the rest.

Having seen the effect of a calving glacier, we were thankful it didn't calve while we were naively resting against the icebergs. In future we thought, it would be wise to stay at least half a mile from the smaller glaciers, and even further from the large ones.

Day 124 15th August

Our stony campsite wasn't conducive to good sleep, and we surfaced early. The day was still and overcast but the cloud base was high and the water of Muir Inlet looked inviting.

The plan was to head up Muir Inlet for nine miles to where Muir Glacier lay, and return to our campsite at Riggs Glacier the same evening. We packed emergency food and a bivvy bag each, just in case, and canoed off, enjoying the feeling of paddling a light boat.

The loose, bare rock of the valley sides loomed steeply to 3,000 feet on either side of us, and occasionally rocks and stones fell, sending amplified echoes down the valley. The ice was no problem in the early stages and only a few well-spaced lumps littered the surface.

Two hours of paddling took us down a straight valley corridor, until we were able to turn a corner and see the imposing wall of Muir Glacier, stretched across the width of the inlet. Floating ice began to appear as we approached the glacier, and scores of seals slithered into the sea for refuge as we approached.

There are over 3,000 seals in Glacier Bay, and one of the main problems of a population as large as that in a relatively small area is the threat of disease, caused by death and the subsequent decay of flesh. An undertaking service is performed naturally for these seals by the hundreds of bald eagles that also live in Glacier Bay.

Half a mile from the glacier we found an area that was clear of ice from where we could watch safely. Muir Glacier was very active, and almost every minute something fell into the sea. The depth of the water in front of Muir Glacier meant that even if a large block fell it sent up a steep swell as opposed to an unfriendly surging breaker.

The glacier had a wide streak of dark brown ice running through the centre. This indicated that it comprised of two glaciers that had merged into one. The dirt and rubble transported from the side of each glacier was now trapped in the middle.

A 150 foot ice pillar leaned precariously over the sea, and we wanted to stay until it fell. Every now and then smaller avalanches of ice fell behind it and beside it, and we knew that it must tumble soon.

Constant creaking and splitting noises accompanied the glacier's pained movements, and suddenly a tremendous crack and rumble signalled the fall of the pillar. It collapsed vertically like a demolished chimney stack, bringing with it a large section of the glacier face. It all disappeared into a white spray with a noise louder than thunder. Slowly, from the depths of the misty spray, a wave came into focus and careered towards us. We paddled back as fast as possible to avoid it and hoped that the floating ice between us and it would stifle it.

Icebergs rolled in its wake but they did the trick and transformed it from a breaking wave to a swell before it reached us. The wave gushed along the valley sides, dislodging rocks in its path, and we rode over the swells, horrified at the thought of nearly having to surf a wave through ice.

A little later the 'Thunder Bay' tour boat arrived with its cargo of sightseers. They stayed at the face of the glacier for about a quarter of an hour, and then headed back to Bartlett Cove. The captain gave us a beer each and one passenger recognised us from Petersberg. On the way back we stopped for a rest on the only available landing spot in the fjord, and we were startled by a big brown swell that washed up the beach without warning for several yards. It would have washed away the kayaks if we hadn't moved them a few minutes earlier and it was incredible to think that it had been caused by ice falling from a glacier over three miles away.

Nearer to our camp at Riggs Glacier, an ocean-going cruise liner steamed slowly up the inlet and even a ship of this size was dwarfed by the grandeur of the glacial scenery. Although it looked out of place, it gave us a graphic idea of the scale of the glaciers and inlets.

Pulling into our camp that evening, another giant lump of ice calved and we only had a minute or so of speedy movement to carry the boats and equipment clear of the danger area. Again it left dozens of ice lumps scattered up the shore.

Day 125   16th August

Remarkably for Glacier Bay it was another clear, calm day but, due to a potential food shortage, we decided to paddle back down the inlet instead of staying for another day.

We reversed our route down the inlet for eighteen miles and all the way the sights were fantastic, with perfect mirror reflections in the milky water.

On the way we passed some remnants of a forest that had flourished in Glacier Bay before the most recent ice age. The vast forests that once grew in the area became engulfed by the morraine of the advancing glaciers thousands of years ago. Under the morraine they remained protected from the abrasive action of the ice and were preserved by the cold. The ice age eventually reached its peak, and then the ice began slowly retreating, in the same manner as it is today. As it retreated it uncovered the morraine, leaving a bare mass of rubble. The morraine, now exposed to the wind and rain gradually eroded, exposing the preserved tree stumps of the forest in the form of interglacial stumps.

We camped on a good beach with plenty of firewood. There had been none further up the inlet, and for the first time all our cooking had to be done on primus stoves.

The vegetation was again quite dense, with alder and immature spruce being the predominant species. Perhaps if the ice advances again, they too may become interglacial forests.

We slept that night with the occasional distant rumble reaching us from ice falling eighteen miles away!

Day 126   17th August

We knew that the outstanding weather wouldn't hold for much longer so we capitalised on it by paddling twenty four miles. We left Muir Inlet and rounded the corner into the main westerly arm of Glacier Bay.

The steep-sided fjord-like character of Muir Inlet had restricted the views of the surrounding mountains, but now we were in the west arm, the bay opened out, and a vast panorama emerged. The Fairweather range, now only twenty or so miles away, formed a jagged white horizon and from our sea level vantage point it was easy to believe that it was the highest coastal range in the world. The patchwork of snow, rock and ice, that formed the peaks and ridges gained heights over 8,000 feet with some reaching in excess of 15,000 feet. Further on, beyond our immediate sight, the range stretched northwestward for hundreds of miles, and upwards to heights of over 18,000 feet.

It was unusual to get such fine mountain panoramas from sea level because normally one has to gain height to get a good view.

Day 127   18th August

During the night the sky clouded over, and we had our first rain for five days. Luckily the wind didn't accompany it, and we had a nice cool paddle, with occasional glimpses of the 5,000 foot peaks on the edge of the sea. Glaciers hung menacingly in the clouds, coming in and out of view between the gently swirling mist.

Nine miles further on we came to Reid Inlet, and saw our next tide water glacier. The two mile deep inlet was calm, but badly choked with small blocks of ice so, to save the tedious task of weaving through the ice at snail's pace, we landed the boats at the mouth of the inlet, and went the rest of the way on foot.

Reid Glacier is not particularly active, but still presents an imposing sight. A section of the snout was above the tidal mark, so we climbed on the rough, crisp surface ice on to the glacier. It was split in all directions by deep, very blue crevasses, and a complex network of smooth-sided ice caves linked the crevasses in a deathly cold maze. Unless properly equipped, a slip from the ice into a crevasse would spell certain death. The cold would numb you from all sides, and the crevasse ice would be too smooth and dense to climb and without the use of a rope, a rescue would be impossible. It was difficult to suppress the urge to climb higher on to the glacier, but the danger and our lack of equipment forced us to retreat. The glacier ice is almost an electric blue and the reason it appears blue, as opposed to transparent like most ice, is that it is so dense that all colours are absorbed except blue. Much can be learned from the colour of the floating ice in relation to the position it held in the glacier.

A navy blue berg comes from near the bottom of the glacier where ice is densest. Green or black ice comes from the bottom of the glacier, where it has been in contact with the ground. Dark stripes indicate that it has been carrying rubble (morraine). White ice contains minute air bubbles, and is far less dense than the blue ice. Clear ice is close to melting, and probably at one stage had been blue ice.

The sound that accompanied the floating ice was a strange fizzing, and popping noise that was caused by the bubbles popping and the ice splitting as it adjusts to a different temperature and pressure. None the less, it still sounded eerie in an otherwise perfectly silent situation.

The depth at which the ice floats in the water depends on its density, the salinity of the water, and the amount of morraine it holds. It has been known for an iceberg to suddenly surge to the surface, having been previously submerged by the weight of morrain it was carrying!

Our camp for the night was on a bed of cotton-topped dryas, near where we had left the boats. A warm fire and a view looking across the ice-choke to Reid Glacier, set the scene for a pleasant relaxed evening together.

Wolf tracks appeared on the beach during supper, but we felt no threat at all from these shy, quiet hunters.

Day 128 19th August

A thick mist and an icy breeze, made canoeing painfully cold on the hands, even wearing our canoe mitts.

We followed a damp, grey-cliffed shore for five miles to Lamplugh Glacier and as we rested in front of the glacier face, three ice columns calved with a terrific roar and splash. Near the glacier was a boulder-strewn beach that looked suitable to land on, so we ran ourselves aground amongst the boulders, and heaved the kayaks up to a safe position. A ridge swept upwards from the beach, and ran roughly parallel with the glacier. Our legs had been virtually redundant for four months, so we decided to drag them up the ridge for a few hundred feet, so that we could see what the glacier looked like from above.

The ridge consisted of loose granite, and every so often we sent down a mini landslide of loose rock. The scale of the glacier became more apparent as we ascended. The lorry-sized icebergs that floated on the dark sea water appeared as tiny pinpricks and Lamplugh Glacier widened as we rose. Other glaciers merged with it from other valleys, creating dark wide streaks in the white ice. It groaned and creaked constantly with fearful intensity, as its straining mass ground its unstoppable course to the sea. We found a wind-sheltered niche high on the ridge to sit in and as we listened to its noise, tried to detect movement.

As we watched, a fishing vessel chugged to the glacier face and tried desperately to dislodge an ice pillar by firing at it repeatedly with a rifle. The bang and the spat as the bullets hit the ice could be heard even from where we were, but nothing fell. After almost twenty minutes of shooting they abandoned their attempt and left. The moment they turned the corner, a tremendous thunder clap reverberated around the bay and a large mass of ice, tumbled from the face, over half a mile from where they had been shooting. Even bullets had no effect on this type of ice, and the glacier, undisturbed, continued its unpredictable retreat.

Later on the mist became heavier and obscured the glacier. We became chilled and descended. Back at the beach we were both too cold to canoe any further, so we camped near the face of Lamplugh Glacier and tried our best to warm up next to a wildly blazing fire.

Day 129   20th August

The weather was truly back on form today, making up for the recent warm spell but despite the biting wind, and the swirling mist our spirits were high, and we felt very privileged to be able to explore the bay at our own pace.

Our aim for the day was to paddle into Johns Hopkins Inlet to see the glacier reputed to be the most active in the bay. From the beach we manoeuvred through the floating ice that had calved from the face of the Lamplugh Glacier, and continued onward into the mouth of Johns Hopkins Inlet.

A few miles into the inlet, the fjord bent sharply to the left, and at this point the ice began to appear. The glacier loomed in the mist, seven miles away, shimmering in a cold haze above a sea of floating ice. Johns Hopkins Glacier was certainly active. Almost constant thunder echoed up the bay and, on two occasions, we saw a splash of brown water rise at the glacier face from over six miles away. The ice became thicker, and the bergs became larger as we paddled nearer and the closer we got the slower we moved, hindered by the quantity of ice. Even the small ice lumps didn't move easily when we tried to nose them out of the way with the kayaks.

Our boats were fairly heavily laden, but the ice blocks were so solid and dense it was almost like running into rocks. The boats took a hammering, as ice ground along the sides, and the paddles chipped each time we punted off the ice in places where we couldn't see the water.

One of the larger ice lumps ahead of us rolled with a clatter, sending up a swell that bounced ice against our boats. Eventually forward progress became painfully slow and fraught with danger, from unpredictable ice collapses. Discretion being the better part of valour, we took a photo and two and a half miles short of Johns Hopkins Glacier we turned around and picked our way out of the chaotic confusion of ice. High in the peaks,, scores of glaciers hung on top of sheer bluffs, and others crept like giant tongues from the valleys. On our way back out of the inlet the ice thinned out, and the mist and rain seemed to thicken proportionately.

On several occasions porpoises and seals spurred us on and kept us company on this bitterly cold August day.

We camped on a beach in Tarr Inlet, just six miles from the largest glacier in the area 'The Grand Pacific'. In the evening a brazen young bald eagle ate a crab, no more than six feet away from us while the horrified adult birds kept their distance.

Day 130 21st August

Surprisingly after a night of buffeting wind, the day dawned clear and still. At the head of the inlet in which we camped lay the Grand Pacific and Margerie Glaciers, spanning the inlet with two and a half miles of ice cliffs. A strong current influenced by the sub-glacial rivers, dispersed the ice very effectively, and despite the huge volumes of ice shed by the glaciers there wasn't the problem of choked seas.

We watched the glaciers for hours, mesmerised by the spectacle of these powerful natural forces at work.

Hundreds of sea birds flew in slow circles close to the glacier face, waiting for icebergs to calve. The violent action of falling ice churns up the bottom and brings crill, shrimps and crab to the surface for what the birds see as an easy feed. Consequently, before the ice collapses, their flight turns immediately from patient grace to mob frenzy, and they follow the falling ice into the watery melée to make the best use of the few moments of turbulence. Some must inevitably get killed, because each major collapse throws out speeding ice 'bricks' for hundreds of feet.

We made our camp near a small grass-covered beach, only a matter of yards from the brown and white veined walls of the Grand Pacific Glacier.

A Cruise Liner in Glacier Bay

The same Liner next to Margerie Glacier

Day 131 22nd August

Glaciers seemed to calve more during the night than during the day. Perhaps this was because the ice melted more during the day allowing the water to creep into the cracks and re-freeze at night prising the precarious ice column apart. Whatever the reason we had very little sleep because of the noise.

In the morning we walked to the glacier face and followed a very fast river of what looked like liquid concrete, to its source. The river erupted with a resonant roar from a deep, tunnel-like hole in the ice, and in its path rolled immense boulders of ice towards the sea. Booming noises sounded above the roar of the water, signalling internal ice falls and the coming of another wave of ice rubble.

The snout of the Grand Pacific lies virtually on the border between Canada and Alaska. This was our furthest point north on the journey, and we were still running parallel with the same Canadian Province we started off in over four months previously!

In the afternoon we paddled alongside the brown streaked face of the Grand Pacific Glacier, to the clean whiteness of Margerie Glacier and spent several more hours watching the marvellous calving of the ice. An ocean-going cruise liner entered the inlet, and as it drew near to the glacier we were able to relate the scale to a familar object. To our surprise, the ice face towered well above the height of the funnels.

Our campsite two miles further on, lay in a position with the Grand Pacific in full view. Both of us were feeling very tired and run down at this stage, but we still felt very close to each other. Despite the obvious rigours of camping for four and a half months we blamed our decrepid state on the food we ate because, apart from a few days immediately after visiting towns, we had been virtually unable to eat dairy products, eggs, green vegetables or meat. A diet such as ours would have been fine for one or two months, but it was definitely insufficient for any longer period.

Day 132 23rd August

On very calm water we headed south east down Tarr Inlet, looking back to catch our last glimpses of the Grand Pacific Glacier through the faint mist that veiled the hills.

Our camera was playing up but not surprisingly, because after five months of a damp and salty atmosphere things inevitably start to seize up. We passed Lamplugh Glacier again, and took a photo in case our previous ones had failed to come out.

By the afternoon we had reached Reid Glacier and set up camp on the same comfortable cotton grass that we had stayed on previously, and were surprised to see that the choke of ice had dramatically dispersed since our visit a few days ago.

An old log made an ideal source of firewood, and we sat all evening by our beach fire looking towards Reid Glacier. This was our last sighting of a tide water glacier on the trip.

Our stay in Glacier Bay could well have been summarised in the words of John Muir, the first naturalist to systematically explore Glacier Bay in 1879. 'These were the highest and whitest of all the white mountains, and the greatest of all glaciers I had yet seen.'

Explorer John Burroughs wrote in 1899 'We saw the world-shaping forces at work, we scrambled over plains that had been built but yesterday. We saw them transport enormous rocks, we saw the remains of extensive forests they had engulfed, probably within the century (actually 7,000 years) and were uncovering again. We saw the beginnings of vegetation in the tracks of the receding glacier, all the while with the muffled thunder of the falling bergs in our ears.' The translation of the Tlingit Indian name for Glacier Bay is 'God dwells here.'

Day 133 24th August

We found it very difficult to get motivated in the morning but once on the water we drew away from Reid Glacier and, in a matter of minutes it was out of sight behind a steep flaking ridge. We paddled fourteen miles before a rapidly strengthening wind forced us to land in a place called Blue Mouse Cove. The wind increased steadily for the rest of the day, bringing with it waves of icy drizzle. The sea picked up and our tent was continually soaked by wind-driven spray that came in short bursts each time a wave broke.

The summer season was drawing rapidly to a close in Alaska and even up to a month ago, trees were turning to their autumn colours. With winter and stormy weather approaching fast, we were aiming to be off the water by the first week in September. With the tide water glaciers behind us, the last 120 mile leg of our journey to Juneau had already begun.

Day 134 25th August

The wind continued to howl all day and the swell grew surprisingly large considering the limited area of sea with which to gain momentum.

In the afternoon we were surprised to see an elderly couple walking along the beach towards us. They were yachtsmen who were also stormed in, and had taken refuge in Blue Mouse Cove. They had smelt the smoke from our fire and had come to investigate. They told us that their ship's barometer had fallen to its lowest pressure for four months and according to local shipping forecasts, the coastal Pacific areas were experiencing hurricane-force winds. Judging by the wind and swell inside Glacier Bay, it was easy to imagine that beyond our protective range of mountains a hurricane was in full swing.

In a way we didn't mind being stormed in because it was an ideal opportunity to rest. The only problem was that we had only enough food for two days, and we estimated that our nearest supply of food was two and a half days canoeing away.

A food check revealed that we only had one quarter of a carrot left, half a potato each, a handful of rice, some sultanas and peanuts. Our main fillers, porridge, grains, flour, sugar, milk and dried vegetables were all gone.

Day 135 26th August

All night the spray from the sea pummelled the tent, and morning saw no improvement in the weather.

We visited the two yachts people in the afternoon and they treated us to tea and biscuits. The shipping forecast did nothing to cheer us, and a continuing storm warning prevailed for the next two or three days.

Before bed a killer whale glided quickly past the beach. Its five foot fin broke surface and knifed through the water three times, until with a final flap of its tail, it sped off underwater and out of sight. That was the first time we had seen the tail fin of an orca rise above the water.

Day 136 27th August

A loud night of crashing waves gave us little sleep, and certainly didn't fortell the sea conditions of the morning.

156

An Ice choked inlet

Kayak silhoetted against the floating ice

By 10am the wind died almost completely, leaving only a choppy swell to hamper progress. The tide, uncharacteristically, was with us, and we covered the eighteen miles to our next campsite with few problems.

We stopped at Johnson Cove to camp, and prepare ourselves for an early morning five mile crossing of the bay. Originally we had hoped to do it all today, but it was touch and go whether we would make it across before dark.

As we pulled into the cove, two canoeists we had met earlier at Riggs Glacier pulled out, and we suggested a good campsite at Flapjack Island for them. Camp for us was set up with the utmost efficiency and the tent was erected, and the fire started in minutes. The boats, now totally devoid of food, were a pleasure to carry and it took us no time to get them up the beach to the high tide mark.

The meal was soon prepared and in seconds supper was over! While contemplating the evening's entertainment, I strolled around the corner for a few yards, and settled into a comfortable squat in what must have rated high on our top forty list of scenic ablution spots.

A rustle of grass thirty yards away shattered the tranquility of the moment, and a black bear burst on to the beach. I leapt up and shouted for Krista to bring a pan. 'What do you want a pan for?' came the reply. 'Just bring one, quick!' She ambled towards me completely oblivious to the urgency in my voice, and then she saw the bear, - it was walking slowly towards us. She quickly picked up a stone and banged the pan furiously, but the bear continued to advance. All the advice we had received along the way to cater for these emergencies went out of the window. I certainly wasn't going to play dead, attack it before it charged, or throw gravel down its throat as people had recommended. We just made as much noise as possible. I took the pan from Krista, and she ran back for another.

We couldn't retreat very far on the island peninsular, so we had to stand our ground. Twenty yards from us it stopped advancing and arched its head towards us. Glad to have achieved a stalemate, we discussed tactics over the din of our pan banging.

Krista was to pack the boats and drag them to the water's edge, while I entertained the bear, and tried to take the tent down.

Krista did marvellously with the packing while I discovered that as soon as I ceased making noise, the bear would take two or three paces closer and only stop when the pan rattling started again. Taking a tent down while rattling a pan takes some doing!!

Soon Krista had done her bit, and came to the rescue. We almost had the tent folded when the bear, who was now only a matter of ten paces away broke the tension and returned to the bushes.

Our meal, although meagre, had attracted it to us, and judging by the rustlings in the trees, the bear was trying to outflank us, and get to our pots and pans by an alternative route. Thanks to Krista's efforts with the boats, a swift sprint down the beach brought us to safety, and we paddled off into the gathering night, just in time to see the puzzled bear re-emerge at the site where the remains of our campfire smouldered.

Such a situation could very easily have turned nasty and considering that a bear can out-run, out-swim and out-climb a man, there was very little else we could have done. Normally bears run a mile if they hear loud human noises. Being in a well-visited National Monument perhaps creates a certain familarity between bears and humans, that could develop into an unhealthy and dangerous lack of mutual respect.

By the time we were halfway across the water, it was virtually dark and our course for Flapjack Island was based on pure guesswork. From sea level at dusk, all the islands and the mainland merged into one, so we estimated our direction, and aimed towards it. By dark the islands were no longer visible, and our only reference point lay in a distant but prominent peak on the mainland that stood out as a dark silhouette against the night sky.

The wind started to blow again, and we knew that this, combined with the tide, would drift us sideways, even if we remained pointing directly at the peak. Maps and compasses were no longer visible and precision had effectively disappeared from our navigation. We hoped that if we paddled in one direction for long enough, sooner or later we were bound to hit land. Our theory proved correct when an hour later I jolted to a dead stop against a rock!

The water in the area was shallow, making it reasonable to assume we were on an area marked foul ground on the nautical chart. We picked our way through the maze of rocks, and at the same time circled to the other side of the island. Visibility was virtually zero, although large rocks and land could vaguely be seen, appearing as darker shades of black than everything else.

We kept tabs on our relative positions by the noise of each other's paddle strokes, and the regular crunching noises as we hit or scraped over rocks.

Three and a half hours after abandoning our last campsite, we landed on the beach of Flapjack Island, and started the camping process again!

Our sleeping bags were occupied by midnight and we were asleep by one minute past.

Day 137 28th August

We were woken by the sound of laughter and discovered that the two kayakers we had met the day before were camped a few yards away!

For breakfast Krista miraculously found some flour and jelly, and promptly invented jelly bread.

The morning passed chatting to Dale and Eric, who had come to the bay for three weeks from Seattle. By midday all four of us were on the water, and we paddled with the wind and tide to Bartlett Cove. Once there we commandeered some potatoes and had an enormous chip session followed by a restaurant meal bought for us by Dale and Eric, for helping to carry their equipment.

All around Bartlett Lodge conversations buzzed about the storm of three days ago and apparently it was a break-away from Typhoon Hollie.

In the bar that evening, as we drooled over a beer, Joan Busby strolled in. What a coincidence!! She was a climber friend from England that we had met a year before. She is in her 70's and every summer goes mountaineering in Alaska. A long conversation with her made our plans for an early night impossible, and we chatted with her into the small hours.

Day 138 29th August

Dale and Eric had flown to Glacier Bay in a plane borrowed from a friend in Seattle, and they were waiting for the right conditions to fly back. Typhoon Hollie was still playing havoc with the weather, and today they were grounded.

I chatted to Dale all day, while Krista and Eric went to the caravan (shop) in Gustavus.

He told me a Tlingit Indian legend that they believe explains the advance and subsequent retreat of the glaciers. The Tlingits were an ancient tribe who inhabited Glacier Bay thousands of years ago, before the ice advanced over it. They retreated in the face of the ice, ending up in Hoonah. A large concentration of Tlingits still live across Icy Strait in Hoonah, and many more are spread all over south east Alaska.

Thousands of years ago when the tribes lived at the head of Glacier Bay, it was customary to send pubescent girls out to live on their own, to keep them chaste until marriage.

One girl became unbearably lonely, so she summoned the glaciers by whistling through fish bones filled with a charm of supernatural powers. The glaciers began to advance and gradually engulfed the village. The villagers retreated again and again, but each time their village became covered by the ice. They crossed Icy Strait and settled again, but the ice continued to advance. The villagers decided that the only way to stop the ice was to sacrifice the girl to the glacier. An old woman stepped forward and said 'she can bear many children and I can bear none, sacrifice me instead.' The villagers agreed and soon the glacier engulfed the old woman's body.

After this, the glaciers started receding, calving off icebergs into the sea. The old lady couldn't bear human children, but the icebergs calving were her ice children.

Day 139 30th August

Dale and Eric were unable to fly again due to the weather conditions. The main coup of the day came when Krista wheeled and dealed with a university camping party for the acquisition of their spare food when they flew home!

The amount of food they left was staggering, and our boats soon became full of goodies again.

Day 140 31st August

After an excellent fry-up, Dale and Eric headed to Gustavus airport, hopefully to fly home.

We met a canoeist called Jason who had just paddled on his own from Anacortes, near Seattle, in two months. He had heard about us from various people he had met en route, including Wally at Baranof Warm Springs.

Jason joined us for supper, and on our way to the Lodge at dusk, we almost walked into the 'Bartlett Cove' bear who was busily eating the contents of the bins he had upset!

A Ranger told us that over the past few weeks it had become too tame for its own good. It had climbed aboard boats and stolen food from the Lodge and campsite. He added that if he gets too dangerous or too familiar with people, sadly, he will have to be shot.

Sometimes bears were given 'people aversion therapy' which roughly translated means a barrel full of buckshot in the backside! Others, for their own protection, get transported by helicopter to destinations hundreds of miles distant, but often this doesn't help; and they find their way back.

Day 141 1st September

This was our last rest day before our final leg to Juneau. In the afternoon we went for a walk through the rain forest to the Bartlett River. The forest was very quiet, with perfectly still Muskeg pools, giving flawless reflections. Moss grew, and water dripped from every branch of every tree and stump. Mushrooms, toadstools and a wide variety of fungus sprouted in all directions. To think that all this area, now fertile with life had been completely bare rocky morraine left by the glacier, only a hundred years before.

When we got back to camp we discovered that a bear had been near our tent, and with its teeth had punctured a tin we had left in the entrance.

There were only two other tents in the forest campsite, but they appeared to be empty.

We spent the evening in the Lodge, hoping the bear would leave the boats alone while we were away to keep them intact for when we leave.

In the dark we left the Lodge, and between there and the campsite we met two people who told us that our tent had been ransacked by a bear. 'How come we get all the fun?' we thought. A little further along the track a gunshot rang out behind us, followed by the squeal of a wounded bear. We found out later it had just had some 'people aversion therapy' for stealing a carrot cake from one of the tour boats.

At the campsite we checked the boats by torchlight, and we discovered to our horror that Krista's kayak was on its side, and equipment had been dragged out on to the beach. In the dim light of the torch we couldn't assess the damage properly, but the boat seemed sound, and only a few tins had been chewed.

At the tent, the bear had opened the front zip, probably accidentally, with its nose, and had dragged everything out into the forest. Our sleeping bags, clothes, papers and passports had been scattered about thirty feet from the tent, in the wetness of the forest. We gathered everything up as best we could and piled it back into the tent, before settling down into a fitful sleep, waiting for the wounded and maybe angry bear to come again.

At this time of the year bears are naturally under a lot of pressure to put on fat for the winter. They are therefore bolder, and also more lethargic. They were not easily scared, and if they did run, it was only for a few yards. One bear, last week, had its dose of bird shot in the bum, ran twenty yards, lay down and fell asleep!

Chapter Eight: **The Homeward Leg**

Day 142 2nd September

The boats were, once again, heavy with food and water, and luckily all our vital equipment was undamaged by last night's bear.

A strong north wind, accompanied by a drizzle, blew very cold, but once out of Glacier Bay, the sea water became noticeably warmer.

In fact, temporary relief from the freezing cold wind was had by dipping our hands into Icy Strait!

We camped at the same spot near Gustavus that we had on the way to Glacier Bay, nearly a month previously.

That evening while we sat next to our fire, a boat pulled up and tied on to the jetty. A burly old Alaskan, sporting a large grey beard, walked up the beach with a net full of salmon. He stopped in his tracks when he saw us, and said 'Hey didn't I see you kayaking at Butedale a few months back?' We didn't recognise him, but we remembered his boat motoring past. They had been fishing, and we overtook them several times as they drifted and chugged on their way up the channel. I looked in my diary and worked out that he had seen us 99 days before. '99 days ago! Well I think that deserves a salmon!' His friend reached into the net and pulled out a huge chunk of ready filleted fresh pink salmon and gave it to us. We exchanged a few stories, and they went on their way, leaving us to settle into a stew, followed by three sessions of fish and chips!

Day 143 3rd September

Considering it had been raining all night, the fire started surprisingly easily in the morning.

A slight north wind blew all day, and snow clouds filled the sky, but all we got at sea level was rain as we retraced our route to Porpoise Island. On the way Mt. Wright, and Beartrack mountains appeared for an instant, giving us our last physical reminder that Glacier Bay was now behind us.

In the distance we could hear the sharp report of a whale slapping its fin, but we couldn't see him in the grey choppy sea. At Porpoise Island we finished off the salmon, with another three fish and chip sessions before an early night.

Day 144 4th September

The day started with a three mile crossing that took us to the mainland shore. We then continued hugging the coast for seventeen miles that took us to our proposed island camp.

Tantalised by the number of salmon that leapt around us, within fifty yards of the shore, we lowered our hooks and trailed them behind the boats. I hooked one huge salmon that leapt and fought extremely hard. Krista had to come alongside to stabilize my canoe as I pulled it in, but once it was alongside us its sheer weight and fight ripped the hook from its mouth and it leapt, flapping vigorously back into the sea.

Moments later Krista caught a more sensibly sized one, but we lost that in the same way. Really we needed a landing net or gaff, because without one they fight hard, and flap too much to control.

Our next idea was to avoid hauling them out of the water, because they only seem to rip free once they were above the surface. Instead, we decided to tow the next one to the nearest landing spot, and haul it straight up the beach. We were sure it would work, but as bad luck would have it, no others took the bait.

At one point, as I sat in the boat winding in the fishing gear, two sea-lions came swimming through the water towards me. I continued winding up the line, thinking they would see me, and alter course before they got too close. Bearing in mind that they can weigh up to 2,000lbs I hoped they would! They were moving fast, and I soon realised that they hadn't seen me and it was too late to move.

The large pale forms surged through the water like torpedoes, gradually rising to the surface for their next breath. They moved so fast I was sure they would hit my boat. I braced myself for impact, when with a sudden gasp they surfaced in unison, with their noses about two feet from the side of my kayak! A split second expression of surprise crossed their faces when they saw me, and with a noisy splash they executed a speedy panic dive, only skimming the underside of my boat. I was glad they did that, because I was half expecting a hard knock, or a leap over the bow! With relief we continued on, watching and following the sea-lions, who seemed to be going the same way as us.

Camp was on a small island, unnamed on our map.

Day 145 5th September

It was too windy to cross to Lynn Canal today so we stayed put on the island for the morning. The canal is a body of water that runs in a north/south direction for sixty miles and is about 10 miles wide at its widest point. In a north wind it becomes notoriously treacherous. It was the fifth day of north winds, so in the afternoon we contented ourselves with a paddle to another island two miles further on to wait for the weather.

In a tide race, Krista caught a good sized halibut which we ate for supper.

The sun came out late in the afternoon and we found a good warm suntrap to sit in, sheltered from the cold wind that whooshed through the trees around us. Wave after wave of migrating geese passed over us, flying in 'V' formation on their route south. Earlier in the trip we had seen them heading north.

Day 146 6th September

An early start enabled us to cross Lynn Canal to the Mansfield peninsular on Admiralty Island, without the hindrance of a strong tide. The air was cold because of the clear night sky, and by the time we had crossed the four miles of water we were ready for breakfast.

The tide had begun to run by the time we were back on the water, and we had to struggle for a few miles until we rounded the tip of Mansfield peninsular. From here until our island camp, we whistled along on the tide, ending up on a very small rocky isle called Barlow Island.

In the evening we saw whales on three occasions, and a large sealion. Juneau was very close now, and in a way it was sad to be so near to the end of our trip.

Day 147 7th September

In the morning the wind still blew briskly, but it didn't deter us from venturing out, as it would have done earlier in the trip.

During breakfast two large humpback whales surfaced several times, close to the sheer-sided reef that fringed our island. We raced over for a closer look and got within thirty feet of them. After three blows for breath, they dived, raising their tails high in the air, and through the fogged-up view finder, Krista got a shot of the final few centimetres of tail before it disappeared for good.

Once on the water, we paddled the two miles to Shelter Island and headed toward Juneau along its southern shore.

Just before the last crossing of our trip, a very strong cross current confronted us, so to avoid the possibility of a long strenuous ferry glide for three miles, we landed and made pancakes on the beach.

Eventually the current slackened and surprisingly the wind dropped, and we paddled four miles to an island well within the Juneau city limits.

Lights of houses surrounded us, and flickered in the trees. Fishing boats chugged by, and others buzzed back to port, returning from their own excursions. Later on the thumping of disco music, and laughter echoed across the water, coming from a neon bar.

The moon rose over the forested hills, and we knew that already we were passing from wilderness into civilisation. The journey was nearly over, and with a feeling of excitement, sorrow and trepidation, our thoughts wandered between adventures past, and the unforseeable future. What would become of us? Two people that had shared an exciting adventure in a wild land? How will we get home, with no money left? Where will we sleep in Juneau?

Do you remember when the whale came up under your boat? or when we camped at the end of the runway? What about the bath on Hot Spring Island? and nearly getting shot in Tenakee Springs? Our adventures, now that they were over, were already just a series of mutual memories. Experiences good and bad that would never be forgotten, always relished, and often thought about.

In the tent that night, we both sifted though our private maze of thoughts, and Krista whispered 'Soon be home.'